The Indo-Germanics

An Outline

by

Gustaf Kossinna

Part 1: The Proto-Indo-Germanics

With 150 Illustrative Figures and 7 Supplementary Maps

Translated by Trevor Sutcliffe

Argent Ardor
2025

Original translation of *Die Indogermanen: Ein Abriss. I. Teil: Das indogermanische Urvolk*
Mannus-Bibliothek No. 26

Published in the United States by Argent Ardor, LLC

Copyright © 2025 Trevor J. Sutcliffe

Translated from the 1st edition published by Curt Kabitzsch, Leipzig, 1921

All rights reserved.

Cover photo: Pottery and axes from Bornholm's Later Stone Age by Lennart Larsen (CC BY-SA). Background expanded with the assistance of generative AI.

ISBN: 9798313413518

Dedicated April 14, 1921 to

Adalbert Bezzenberger

in long and lasting friendship.

To you, my highly esteemed friend!

I'm not particularly fond of bulky or even multi-volume scholarly works, neither as a reader nor as a writer, and having reviewed your works, I believe that you and I are of one mind in this respect. One can also communicate a boundless amount in the form of a terse outline, both in terms of summarizing older information as well as one's own newly generated material. And given the current conditions in German economic life, especially in the book publishing trade, narrowly limiting one's presentation to what is scientifically indispensable is also an external commandment one must strictly observe. That is why, a year ago, I endeavored to present my current position on the "Indo-Germanic question" to the linguistic circles in one of their journals in the briefest outline, which I'd intended to not even fill a printer's signature. The essay was already prepared when, after several unforeseen circumstances, I felt compelled to publish it separately. I meanwhile had the advantage of being able to furnish it with numerous illustrative figures which I had been reserving for other purposes. In order to explain said figures, however, the text required extensive augmentation. And so, in the space of two months, this essay grew to five printer's signatures worth of material. These augmentations have almost exclusively been to the benefit of the archaeological illumination of the Indo-Germanic question, while the linguistic and anthropological sections have remained limited to those standpoints contained in the brief first draft, as I did not have the time to dress up these skeletons with additional flesh and blood. For in the meantime I had decided that this should be a commemorative publication for an occasion which was only a few weeks away. This writing deals especially with the neighbors of the Indo-Germanics in Europe, and since the ethnic conditions in Western Europe during the Stone Age are still unclear, it is primarily limited to Central, Northern, and Eastern Europe. Eastern Europe probably occupies the broadest space in this presentation. To whom, then, could I with more justification dedicate this work than you, my dear friend, who with great care, and in what unfortunately was a hitherto unprecedented way, has so affectionately combined the cultivation of Indo-Germanic linguistic research with the cultivation of prehistoric and early historic archaeology, and, in both, primarily to the benefit of the Eastern European regions? And then there is the fact that you are turning seventy, which releases you from the obligation, but certainly not the right, to continue teaching at the venerable Albertina. May you be granted many more years of undiminished physical vitality to devote yourself to the fulfillment of the scientific accomplishments which you have set out for yourself as a goal.

With heartfelt admiration,
your faithful friend,
G. Kossinna.

Contents.

	Page
I. Linguistic Research and Original Homeland.	1–4

"Oak," "Beech," and "Yew" 1. — Types of Vegetables 2. — "Bear" and "Bee" 3. — "Eel" and *"Lachs"* 3. — "Sea" 3. — Copper: *Ajasja* 4. — κασσίτερος and πέλεκυς 4. — Seasons 4. — "Woad"; Turtle 4.

II. Racial Research	5–7

Three major racial strains in Europe 5. — Western European racial strain: short-headed Jura branch, long-headed Nordic branch 5. — Finnics 7. — Lapps 7.

III. Proto-Finns and Proto-Indo-Germanics	7–10

Primordial affinity between the Finnic and Indo-Germanic languages 7. — Finnic as a branch of Uralic 7. — Early development of root stress and consonant gradation in Uralic 8. — Proto-Finnic and Proto-Lappish have Proto-Germanic loanwords from the 1st millennium BC, and before that already had Baltic loanwords, and even earlier, Indo-Iranic loanwords 9. — Seats of the Proto-Finns and Pre-Finns since 2000 BC 9.

IV. Archaeology	10–79
1. The Emergence of the Proto-Indo-Germanics	10–35

Immigration of Western Europeans to northern Germany since the occurrence of the "Baltic" end moraines: Reindeer antler implements 10. — Geological profile of the sites of archaeological finds 11. — Yoldia period of the Baltic Sea: almond-shaped flint implements 13. — The Ancylus stage 14. — Skulls of the Ancylus period 15. — The "Dobbertin" people 20. — Hunting and fishing implements of the Dobbertiners made out of bone and antler 20, out of flint 22. — Language of the Dobbertiners 26. — The Littorina stage 27. Skulls of the Littorina population 27. — The "Ellerbek" people 28. — Better flint implements 29. — The first ceramic vessels 30. — The Pre-Indo-Germanics 31. — Colonial areas in northeastern France and southeastern England 31. — Eastern European contingent, Sumerians (?) 33. — Later shell middens; agriculture, animal husbandry; Language = Indo-Germanic 33. — Land pile-dwellers = Ligurians (?) 34.

Page

2. The Emergence of the Pre-Finns and Their Retreat from the Indo-Germanics 35–60

Persistence of the Dobbertin civilization in Sweden: the Lihult-Nøstvet rock axes 35. — The round-butted axes 37. — The earlier "Arctic" Dwelling-Place civilization = Pre-Finns 37. — Their animal sculptures 39. — Their implements 40. — Statistical investigation of the occurrence of the various Stone Age implements found in particular Swedish landscapes to determine the first settlement of these environments 40. — Amalgamation of the Pre-Finns with the Indo-Germanics 44. — Anthropological evidence for this amalgamation 46. — Anthropology of Denmark's Stone Age population 48. — Likewise for the Bronze and Iron Ages 50. — Likewise for the contemporary times 51. — Retreat of the Pre-Finns to northern Sweden, their slate industry 52. — Further retreat to central Norway and eastern and northern Finland 53. — In southwestern Finland, the Finno-Indo-Germanic Boat Axe civilization 55. — Final backflow of Pre-Finnic influences from Finland and Karelia to Scandinavia 57.

3. Pre-Finns and Proto-Finns in Eastern Europe 61–75

"East Finnic" pottery: its origin and expansion 61. — Fatyanovo civilization 63. — Their formation: Pre-Finnic and Northern Indo-Germanic 70. — Tocharians as a Thracian branch, Hittites as Northern Indo-Germanic 71. — The potential source of their emigration to Asia Minor 72. — The Copper civilization of eastern Russia 73. — They are Pre-Finnic and are ancestral to the Proto-Finns 74.

4. The First Cleavage of the Proto-Indo-Germanics 75–79

The point-butted and the thin-butted flint axe 75. — Large stone tombs, arguably an influence from Ireland, adopted only by the Indo-Germanics, not by the Pre-Finnic inland Jutlanders 75. — Under the influence of the Indo-Germanics, the inland Jutlanders became Finno-Indo-Germanics during the Dolmen period, but became a culturally independent people again during the Passage Grave period 78. — At the beginning of the Dolmen period, a segment of the Proto-Indo-Germanics branched off towards the central Danube, where the hearth of the Southern Indo-Germanics was established 78.

V. Table 80–81
VI. Supplements 82–83

As a result of my own and other researchers' constantly renewed, ever more intensive examination of the immense, already-existing archaeological material, and especially as a result of significant recent archaeological discoveries, but also as a result of the progress of racial and linguistic research, not only have my earlier views on the Indo-Germanic question of 1895[1] and 1902[2] long since become antiquated, but those of 1908[3] and, consequently, their continuation of 1911[4] have also become in need of revision on certain essential points.

I. Linguistic Research and Original Homeland

According to Hoops[5], the Indo-Germanic cognates for the names of "oak" prove Europe to be the original Indo-Germanic homeland, those for the names of "beech" and "yew" notably only to the area west of the Königsberg-Odessa line, and finally the preferred status of barley as the most ancient nutrient grain speaks for Northern Europe in conjunction with northern Germany. The cognates for "flax" were erroneously doubted by Hoops, simply because there were still no flax finds in the Nordic region from the Stone Age. In Denmark, however, it has now been proven that flax was a material that has been preserved from an early stage of the large stone tombs, namely the time of the transition from the dolmens to the passage graves, that is, around 3000 BC. For at a Stone Age site near Svendborg on Funen, half of the neck of a globular flask (Fig. 1) was found, which was made from a hollowed-out bull's horn and covered on the outside with three layers of tightly woven flax thread that had been diagonally wound around one another. This braiding served to connect the neck of the vessel to the belly of the vessel, which was made of some other material, perhaps wood or leather: such

---

[1] Kassel Germanic Lecture: *Zeitschrift des Vereins für Volkskunde*. Berlin, 1896, pp. 1 ff.
[2] "Die indogermanische Frage archäologisch beantwortet": *Zeitschrift für Ethnologie*. 1902, pp. 161 ff.
[3] "Urfinnen und Urindogermanen": *Mannus* I. II. 1909–10.
[4] *Die Herkunft der Germanen*, Würzburg 1911; 2nd Ed. Leipzig 1920.
[5] Johannes Hoops: *Waldbäume und Kulturpflanzen im germanischen Altertum*. Strasbourg 1905.

wooden vessel bellies (without necks) from Denmark are well-documented. The most outwardly visible diagonal threads are crossed in a perpendicular direction by other threads, alternately above and below, such that the whole weave corresponds exactly to the kinds of threads that were at that time, and only during that brief time period, pressed into the still moist clay of the sides of these vessels as a decorative motif. So the leftover flax thread that was fortuitously preserved here was not an exception, but something that had been commonplace[1].

As I have often emphasized, I am generally not open to negative evidence

Interior.   Exterior.

Fig. 1: ¹/₁. Svendborg, Funen (per Aarbøger for nordisk Oldkyndighed 1913).

from linguistic research, which is always rather unreliable in any individual case. One exception, however, can be made for the names of types of vegetables, for which there are no common Indo-Germanic cognates. Here, the absence of the entire group of names lends a certain reliability to the negative evidence, especially since archeology has hitherto proceeded hand-in-hand with linguistic research. The lands south of the Danube must therefore be excluded as candidates for the original homeland.

---

[1] *Aarbøger for nordisk Oldkyndighed og Historie* 1913, p. 272.

The Indo-Germanic names for "bear" and "bee" attest to Europe; whether the names for "eel" and *"Lachs"* (salmon)[1] can be proven to indicate Northern Europe does not strike me as entirely certain. However, Otto Schrader's objection on the grounds that the eel has actually recently been caught on a number of occasions in the Black Sea is invalid, as we know that eel broods have recently been widely released in the uppermost Danube by fish farmers.

In contrast, the Indo-Germanic cognates for *"Meer"* (sea) point to the North Sea and the Baltic Sea, not to the Black Sea or the Caspian Sea. The fact that the Italics call the sea *mare*, while the form *more* would be consistent with their sound laws, could perhaps be explained by the fact that (on account of the amber or fur trade?) the word was constantly supplied to this tribe in its original seats in inland Central Europe by its Germanic neighbors. However, standing in the way of such a conjecture is the fact that the Germanic sound change ŏ>ă only seems to have taken place during the last century before Christ (*Mosa* = Maas, *Vosagus* = Wasgau). In the Latin *mare*, therefore, one must recognize an influence from the Illyric (Albanoid) side. The Greek ϑάλαττα is a loanword from Phoenician from the 10th to the 8th century BC, the time of the short-lived flowering of Phoenician world trade in the Mediterranean[2] and naval transport to and from Tartessos: out of *Taršisch*, the Greeks made *Tarath, Talath*[3]. Such a borrowing would scarcely have occurred had the Greeks migrated to the Balkan Peninsula from an original homeland on the Black Sea, whereby they would have never lost contact with the sea. But the matter becomes quite comprehensible if the Greeks had lost all vital connection with seafaring during their long journey from the Baltic Sea to the Aegean Sea, and had only regained familiarity with seafaring, maritime commerce, and overseas colonization while under the tutelage of the Phoenicians.

The fact that the Greeks adopted new words for important cultural objects instead of continuing to use their ancestral ones after losing their closer connection with the main body of the Northern Indo-Germanics and coming into close contact with non-Indo-Germanics in Greece and the Near East can also be seen in other ways. For instance, they now called copper χαλκός, while the Indics,

---

[1] In addition to Germanic, Lithuanian, and Russian, the word "Lachs" is also found in Tocharian, while the Celts and Italics used to call this fish *esox*, and the Gaulish word *salm* was probably derived from the Iberian (Aquitani) one. See Julius Pokorny in: *Berichte der Forschungs-Institutes für Osten*, Bd. III, 1919, S. 27.

[2] Kossinna: *Die deutsche Vorgeschichte: eine hervorragend nationale Wissenschaft*, 2nd Ed. p. 17.

[3] Julius Oppert: *Zeitschrift für Ethnologie* 1903, pp. 212 ff. For our purposes it does not come into consideration that the ancient *Taršiš* was originally located on the Persian Gulf and would only later be bundled together with the Spanish Tartessos. (Georg Hüsing: *Orientalische Literaturzeitung* 1907, Col. 26 f.).

Iranics, Italics, and Germanics (and probably the rest of the Northern Indo-Germanics as well, although we cannot verify this) stuck with the ancient loanword *ayas, ayanh, aes, aiz*, which was derived from the ancient name of the copper-rich island Cyprus, *Ajasja* (earliest evidence around 1467 BC), even more anciently *Alasja*, in which the l represented such an indefinite breath sound that its Indo-Germanic borrowers could immediately render it as a j[1].

Further evidence for this are the loanwords κασσίτερος "tin," and perhaps also πέλεκυς "axe." Both words come from the Near East, the first from an Elamite language, the second from Sumerian (Babylonian), and these were only adopted by the Greeks and the Indics (*kastira* and *paraçu*-)[2]. Later, when the gaze of the Greeks was no longer exclusively directed towards the Orient, but increasingly began to turn toward the west of the Mediterranean region, they transposed not only the Amazons of the Crimea, the Hesperides, and the Ethiopians of Elam[3] to the west, but also the Pillars of Hercules, that is, the altars of Melqart, from Aden on the Red Sea to Gibraltar, as well as the island of Kassitira beyond those altars, that is, according to Hüsing, the ore-rich island of Hormuz near the Persian Gulf, to the westerly ocean upon their discovery of a new source of tin there.

The concordance of the Indo-Germanic designations for only three seasons, namely spring, summer, and winter, as well as for "snowing," likewise speaks to an original homeland of a more northerly location[4].

As for Otto Schrader's[5] opinion that the Indo-Germanic cognates for the "woad" plant and for the "turtle" speak against Northern Europe as the original homeland, I have long since demonstrated that this is completely erroneous[6].

---

[1] Georg Hüsing: Memnon I, p. 213; III, p. 90; *Wiener Zeitschrift für die Kunde des Morgenlandes* 23, p. 414; Julius Pokorny: *Zeitschrift für vergleichende Sprachforschung* 49, pp. 126 ff.

[2] Hüsing: *Orientalische Literaturzeitung* 1907, Col. 25; Julius Pokorny: *Zeitschrift für celtische Philologie* Bd. 9, pp. 164 f.; 12, pp. 305 f.; — The idea proposed by Salomon Reinach that κασσίτερος is a Celtic word (*L'Anthropologie* 1892, p. 275), which has almost universally found favor with Celtic linguists, is a total absurdity.

[3] Hüsing: *Mitteilungen der Anthropologischen Gesellschaft in Wien* 1916. 46, p. 200.

[4] Johannes Schmidt: "Die Urheimat der Indogermanen und das europäische Zahlensystem." Berlin 1890 (*Abhandlungen der Berliner Akademie der Wissenschaften*).

[5] Otto Schrader: *Sprachvergleichung Und Urgeschichte: Linguistisch-Historische Beiträge Zur Erforschung Des Indogermanischen Altertums*. 3rd Ed. Jena 1907.

[6] *Mannus* IX, pp. 114 f. — Recently, again in the north-east corner of the Altmark, in Thüritzberg, district of Osterburg, a Stone Age shallow grave featuring a crouched burial was uncovered, which belongs to the "Rössen" civilization, and which contained among the grave goods the back shell of a male pond turtle; see *Beiträge zur Geschichte Landes- und Volkskunde der Altmark* Bd. IV, Heft 6, Stendal 1920, pp. 335 f., Fig. 3. — [See Supplements on p. 82.]

II. Racial Research

Great progress has been made here thanks to the insights of Karl Felix Wolff, insofar as the formerly dominant belief in the uniformity and the Asiatic origin of the European short-headed race has proven to have been erroneous[1]. Rather, we have three major racial strains in Europe: firstly, a Western European one, commonly called Nordic or Northern European, which is split into the Nordic longhead branch and the West Alpine or Jura shorthead branch, both of which are blond, long-faced, and narrow-nosed, with the former being tall, and the latter medium-to-tall. Secondly, an Eastern European racial strain that is split into the long-headed Ryazan branch with a pear-shaped skull, which includes the southeastern Great Russians and the Finno-Ugrians of the Volga and Urals, and the short-headed Carpathian-Sudeten branch, which includes most of the remaining Slavic tribes: both of which are brunet, broad-nosed, small-to-medium sized, and which probably originated in the southeast of European Russia. Thirdly, the Southern European racial strain, whose long-headed branch includes the Semites and the "Mediterranean race," and whose short-headed branch is represented by the short-headed Syriac-Armenoid type (which encroaches into the Balkan Peninsula).

In the case of the Indo-Germanic race, we are dealing primarily with the Western European racial strain, both branches of which acquired their light pigmentation under the influence of the humid Ice Age climate north of the Pyrenees and Alps in France, southern England, the Rhineland, and in the region of the upper Danube. The distribution of the Nordic longhead branch across Scandinavia, Denmark, Finland, the Baltic lands, Scotland, England, Central Europe, and northern France is well known. Fig. 2 shows a Nordic longhead in the side, top, and rear views. The short-headed Jura branch resides in eastern France, the western Alps, Brittany, Belgium, on the Dutch and Norwegian coasts, in Jutland, northeastern Germany, southern Sweden, Finland, and in the region of the Valdai. An exemplification of the Jura branch can be seen in the picture of a skeleton of a miner from the Early Neolithic period, who was buried by collapsing rubble while he was extracting the flint nodules from underground chalk layers with a two-handed pickaxe made of deer antlers (Fig. 3). The skeleton

---

[1] K. F. Wolff: "Kann die sogenannte alpine Rasse asiatischer Herkunft sein?" (*Archiv für Rassen- und Gesellschafts-Biologie* 1913 X, Heft 6). — See K. F. Wolff: *Politisch-anthropologische Monatsschrift* XIII, 1914, No. 9, 10; XIV, 1915, No. 5, 6; XVII, 1918. — See also Kossinna: *Mannus* 11/12, p. 254 ("Höhepunkte nordindogermanischer Kultur").

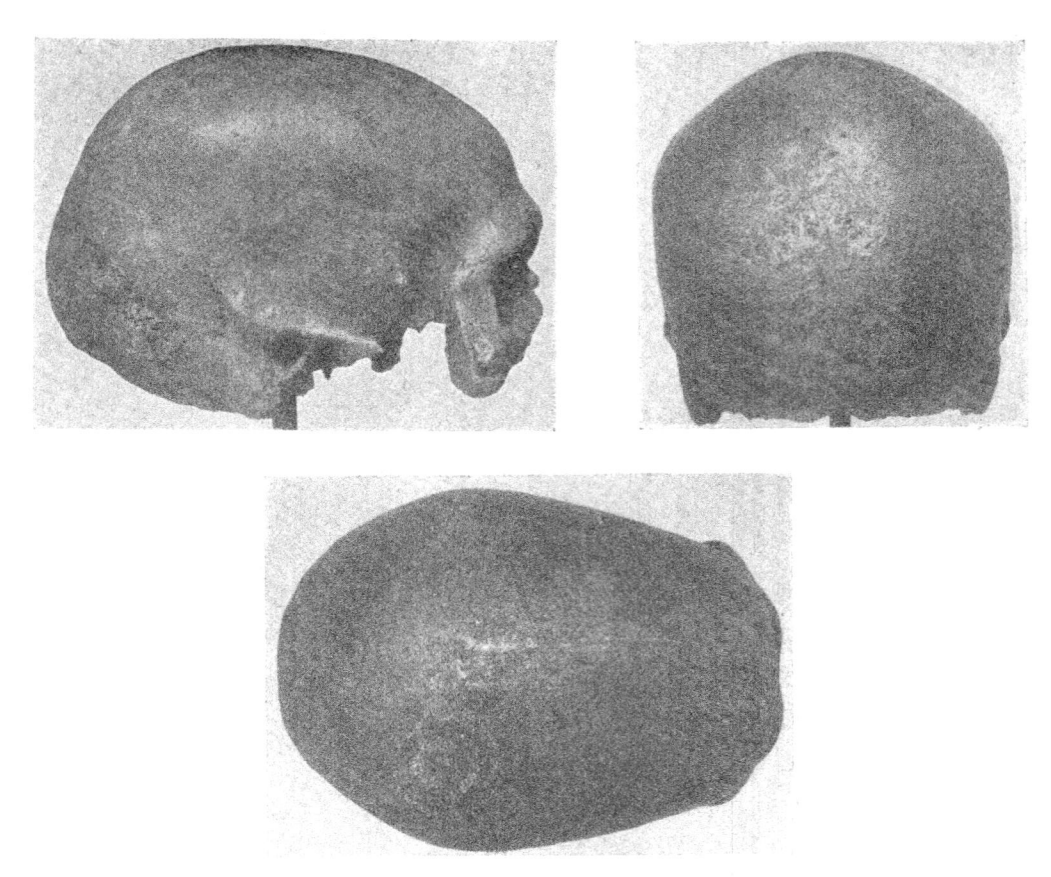

Fig. 2: Approximately ⅓. Friesack, Kreis Westhavelland. Former collection of Georg Hintze, Friesack. Nordic longhead of 185:135 length/width measure; cephalic index 73. Found together with arm and leg bones, numerous flint implements, 2 antler implements, and 1 bone implement.

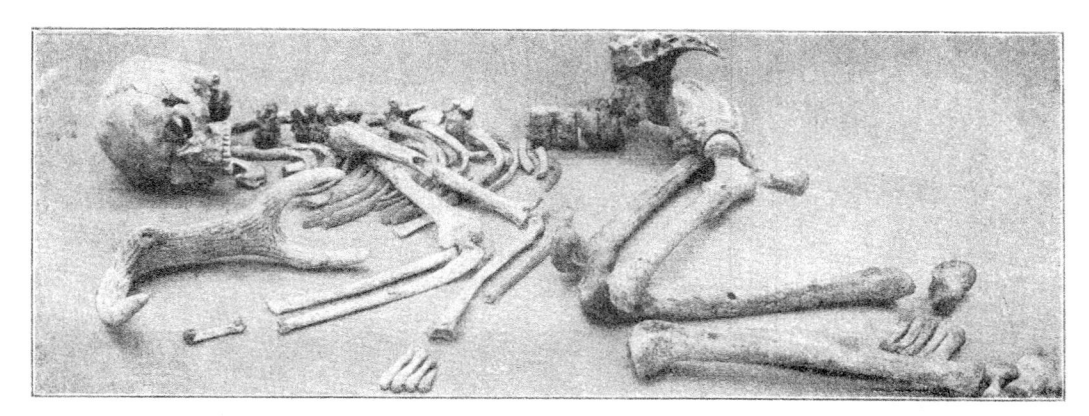

Fig. 3: Miner's skeleton, Obourg, Belgium (per Kossinna, *Mannus* I).

is 1.55 meters tall, and the skull has a cephalic index of 80. A map of the distribution of the measured Neolithic skulls in France and Belgium shows that the short-headed skulls appear as early as the Later Stone Age, particularly in eastern France and Belgium, and occasionally in Brittany (see the map on p. 84).

The Finnics in Finland belong partly to the long-headed and partly to the short-headed branch of the Western European racial strain; the short-headed Jura branch is particularly prevalent in the Valdai Hills[1]. According to the investigations of F. W. Westerlund[2], the West Finns in "Finland Proper" are predominantly long-headed, with a mean cephalic index of 79.4, while towards the east and north the short-headedness increases, and in Karelia the mean index is 82.2, while in northern Ostrobothnia it reaches 82.6. According to Deniker[3], the Estonians are "almost long-headed," the Cheremis (the Mari, near Kazan on the Volga) "approximately long-headed," and the East Finnic Ugrians in general "approximately short-headed." We will return to this in the next section (p. 8). — The Lapps, who must also be mentioned here, speak a West Finnic language which, according to Heinrich Winkler, has been grafted onto an East Finnic (Ugric) language, and they do not belong to the Western but to the Eastern European racial strain, namely to a geographically separate, particularly short-statured variety of the short-headed Sudeten type.

III. Proto-Finns and Proto-Indo-Germanics

Linguistic research has recently placed the original homeland of the Proto-Finns towards European Russia in the area between the Baltic Sea and the Urals. Finno-Ugric is the main branch of the Uralic language family, which also includes Samoyed. Nothing is scientifically certain about the previously accepted relationship between the Uralic languages and the Ural-Altaic languages (Turkic languages, Mongolian)[4]. According to Wiklund, Finnic has undergone only a slight amount of development over the past two millennia. The affinity that Proto-Finnic and even Uralic as a whole share with Proto-Indo-Germanic is an established fact, which is first of all proven by the primordial affinity of the mutual designations for "water," "fish," "raven," "borer," "dwelling-pit," "dwelling-cone," (above the dwelling-pit), "morning twilight," and "name." The

---

[1] Ethyme Tschepourkovsky: "Anthropologische Studien" (*Archiv für Anthropologie* 38, 1911).
[2] Fennia 18, 20, 21, 1900–1904.
[3] J. Deniker: *Les races de l'Europe*. Paris 1899, pp. 84 ff.
[4] K.B. Wiklund: *Le Monde Oriental* IX. 1915.

affinity between Finno-Ugric alone (therefore excluding Samoyedic) and Indo-Germanic is demonstrated by the highly similar words for "honey" and "salt."[1] In particular, the similarity of the personal, demonstrative, relative, and interrogative pronouns is striking. The following features also correspond: inflection through suffixation (agglutination in Finno-Ugric cannot be derived from this!); nominal stem-forming suffixes; stem-forming and inflection through reduplication; ablaut; and the absence of grammatical gender. The primordial stage of Uralic also included the intricate grammatical cases involving the weakening of the stem consonant before a subsequent accent, which some time ago was named *"Stufenwechsel"* (consonant gradation) by Thomsen. For Germanic, the onset of the effects of the so-called Verner's law involved something very similar. And that "Stufenwechsel" also has the stress of the root as precondition, which has already been demonstrated as a feature of Uralic, just as it, in turn, became one of the most prominent characteristics of Germanic as opposed to Indo-Germanic. However, it has not yet been established (as Wiklund has informed me in written correspondence) how far back we can trace the usual common cases in most Finno-Ugric languages of the musical pitch and expiratory heavy stress of the root syllables of words.

All of these close, primordial linguistic affinities between Proto-Finns and Proto-Indo-Germanics, although only shared in part with the Proto-Germanics, are complemented by the original parity of the racial affiliation of both peoples, which lay within the Western European racial strain, and which was only significantly impaired in the case of the greater part of the Finno-Ugrians as a result of the later dispersal of the "Pre-Finns" from Scandinavia and Finland into Eastern Europe and still further eastward due to the pronounced absorption of Eastern European and even Mongoloid racial traits, such as a considerable width of the cheek and chin bones and a darker color of hair[2].

---

[1] K.B. Wiklund: *Le Monde Oriental* I. 1906.

[2] Even Heinrich Winkler, who sees the prehistory and ancestry of the Finno-Ugrians quite differently than I do, also emphasizes blondness and blue-eyedness as the basic trait of the purer components of all Finnic tribes, even among the East Finnic Lapps and Ostyaks, although theirs is of a somewhat darker shade, and he also mentions the still numerous occurrences of long-skulledness, even among the East Finnic Voguls (though not among Ostyaks and Lapps): *Orientalisches Archiv* 1, 1910/11. H. 3, especially p. 119, p. 124 ("Die mongoloiden Völker Europas und die Basten"). — According to Jean N. Smirnov (*Les Populations Finnoises des Bassins de la Volga Et de la Kama. Traduites du Russe Et Revues par Paul Boyer*. Paris 1898), the Mordvins consist of a blond, light-colored tribe and a brunet, dark-colored tribe. The same applies to the Magyars, who are still essentially pure, especially in the Great Hungarian Plain, and who are also characterized by blond-to-brown hair and very light, mostly straw-yellow beard hair, and very frequently by gray-blue eyes,

The Proto-Finnic and Proto-Lappish of the linguists goes back to at least the first half of the first millennium BC, since the oldest Proto-Germanic loanwords of these two languages, which were adopted before the completion of the Germanic sound shift, must come from this time at the latest. According to Wiklund[1], this is demonstrated by the Finnish *rauta*, the Norwegian-Lappish *ruovdde* "iron," and the Old Norwegian *raudi* "bog iron ore." Around this time, the Proto-Finns (that is, the Finnics of the Baltic Sea in tandem with the Lapps) and the Proto-Germanic peoples must have been in close proximity, be it in Finland or in northern Scandinavia. However, according to Vilhelm Thomsen[2] and especially E. N. Setälä[3], before the period of borrowings of Germanic words came a period of Baltic (Lithuanian-Lettish) borrowings, in which the Volga Finns also took part, and even earlier was the period of Proto-Iranic borrowings, which applied to all Finno-Ugrians, and which could only have occurred around the time when a common Indo-Iranic language was still largely preserved, so to be precise, when the Proto-Indics were already in the Caucasus, but the Proto-Iranics were still a unified people that had been left behind in southern Russia. This puts us at least as far back as 2000 BC, and probably even earlier, if today's linguistic research is correct in dating the crossing or circumvention of the Caucasus by the Proto-Indics at around 2500 BC. At that time, segments of the Finno-Ugrians had advanced from Finland and northern Russia into central or even southeastern Russia.

During the second or toward the beginning of the first millennium before Christ, the Proto-Finns in the narrower sense must have separated from the Ugrians and Permians and moved in close proximity to the Lithuanian-Lettish peoples. Some time later, but still in the first half of the first millennium BC, the West Finns struck out independently (in tandem with the Lapps, who were already linked to them at that time) without the Volga Finns and migrated into the realm of the Germanics, that is, back into the vicinity of the prehistoric hearth from which they had originated, where by this time rather than Indo-Germanic

---

but also, just like the Finns, by a yellow, conspicuously wrinkled, lean face at a very young age, especially among the female sex: Heinrich Winkler, "Das Finnentum der Magyaren" (*Zeitschrift für Ethnologie*. Berlin 1901. Bd. 33, pp. 167 ff.). For an account of the frequent long-skulls of the Proto-Magyars, see also *Verhandlungen der Berliner Gesellschaft für Anthropologie* 1896, pp. 499 f.

[1] *Indogermanische Forschungen* 30, pp. 48 ff. 1917.
[2] Thomsen: *Beröringer mellem de finske og baltiske Sprog*. Copenhagen 1890.
[3] Setälä: "J. N. Smirnows Untersuchungen über die Ostseefinnen" (*Journal de la Société Finno-Ougrienne* 17, 1900).

or Finno-Indo-Germanic, Germanic was already being spoken.

How do the Fennologists, especially Wiklund, now intend to explain the ancestral kinship that they have established between Indo-Germanic and Uralic, if they place the original homeland of the "Uralians" on both sides of the Urals and then calmly lay down their pens and abandon any further contemplation? In the case of Uralic, one must seek the connection with Indo-Germanic by looking westward and back into the earlier ages, just as it has been necessary for me to do (quite independently of this), and it is there that one is able to connect a low-level, almost progressless civilization of a fisher and hunter people in Scandinavia and eastern Finland, who were in constant retreat further north and then into northeastern Europe as they retreated from the superior Indo-Germanic civilization, with the Proto-Finns. In order to distinguish these purely archaeologically determined Finnics of the Stone Age from the purely linguistically determined Finnics of the last millennium before Christ, I gladly cede to the Fennologists the moniker of "Proto-Finns," which I had introduced into archaeological science in 1908, and henceforth I shall refer to these Stone Age Finnics as the "Pre-Finns."

IV. Archaeology
1. The Emergence of the Proto-Indo-Germanics

After the final melting of the Ice Age glaciers in northern Germany on the Baltic Ridge, there was one last glacial standstill, which is called the Fourth Ice Age or the Baltic Ice Age (Baltic end moraines)[1] (see the map on p. 85), and from about 15,000 BC swarms of people of the Western European racial strain emigrated from the Upper Rhine region[2] to northern Germany[3]. Evidence of this

---

[1] These end moraines, called *"daniglazial"* in Sweden, run from the Swedish west coast through Scania to Elsinore, over the northwest coast of Zealand and the south coast of Furen to Apenrade, Flensburg, and Schleswig, then southeast through Holstein, across Lübeck, Waren, Neustrelitz, Joachimsthal, and Oderberg, then east and northeast across Soldin, Berlinchen, Nörenberg, Dramburg, Konitz, and so on.

[2] As early as 1908, Austria, here really only meaning Moravia, could no longer come into question for me as having been region of the homeland of this earliest northern German population, since the Magdalenian people there lacked the harpoons for fishing, which are well represented in the Rhine area and on the uppermost Danube. This puts an end to Almgren's doubts as to whether Austria should instead be considered (in Isidor Flodström: *Sveriges folk*. Stockholm. 1918, p. 19).

[3] I have dealt more fully with the Early Neolithic period and the non-Indo-Germanic civilizations and populations of the Late Neolithic period of Northern Europe in *Mannus* I, 1909, pp. 23-52; see also my lecture "Höhepunkte nordindogermanischer Kultur" (*Mannus* 11/12, 1920, p. 249 ff.).

is found in the increasingly numerous implements made of reindeer antlers[1], which have been extracted from the clay pits of the Havel, and which belong to the archaeological period of the Late Magdalenian. We are still awaiting a definitive explanation as to what the geological conditions were under which such clays were formed in certain regions immediately after the melting of the ice. In general, it has been established that at the bottom of the lakes left behind by the

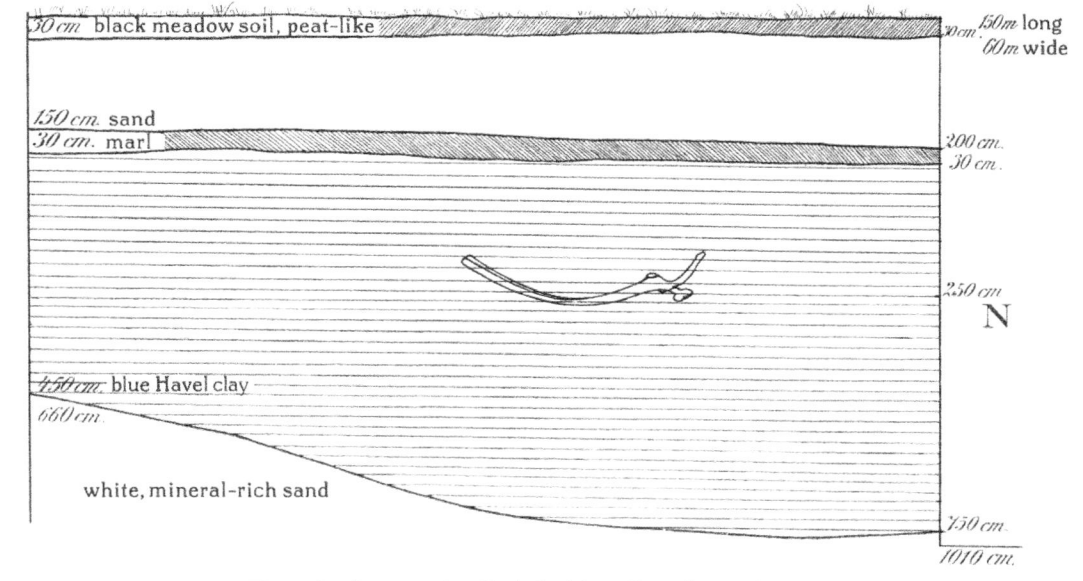

Fig. 4: Großwusterwitz, Kreis Jerichow II, major sections.

Ice Age, accumulations of lime mud or freshwater marl, which are usually called lacustrine chalk or "meadow limestone," were formed by the deposition of calcareous components. In the lowest layers of this meadow limestone, reindeer antlers are found in some areas of northern Germany, but in somewhat higher layers of the same meadow limestone, we find bone and antler implements from the following geological-archaeological period, the Ancylus period (see p. 14). River sands or river gravel are usually found above the meadow limestone, with peat or bog soil above them. In the Havel area, however, thick layers of blue clay are found under the meadow limestone, and sometimes instead of it; these are quarried by the brickworks, whereby the bone and antler implements in question are unearthed. The strata of the rock bed are listed here from top to bottom, as follows (see Fig. 4):

---

[1] Richard Stimming: *Mannus* VIII, 1916, pp. 233 ff.

1. Peat or bog soil
2. River sands and river gravel
3. Meadow limestone
4. Havel clay
} alluvial deposits

5. Sand and Gravel: diluvial deposits

Found in the clay of the Havel were shed antlers from reindeer, which show evidence of pieces having been carved out of them so that they could be processed further, as well as handled axes (Fig. 5) and pickaxes (Fig. 6), and thick lance points or daggers of solid or, more rarely, hollow split

Fig. 5: Briest an der Havel, Kreis Westhavelland. Handled reindeer antler axe.

Fig. 6a b: Pritzerber See, Kreis Westhavelland. Reindeer antler pickaxe. a) from the front, b) from the side.

reindeer antlers (Fig. 7). Similar axes and pickaxes were also found in Schleswig-Holstein and Denmark (Fig. 8). Ever since Gustav Stimming (the father) of Brandenburg wrote in 1887 that among the bone spearheads and harpoons in his collection, which come from the Havel clay, there were also some that were made from reindeer antlers or reindeer bones, this assertion has become more and more established in the literature and has lately been applied to more and more

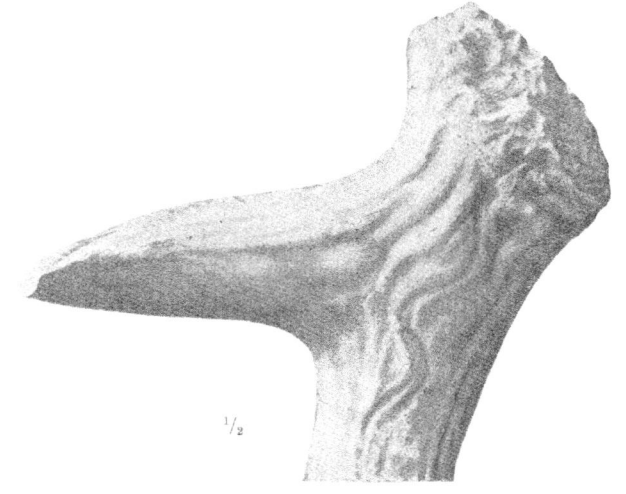

Fig. 6c: Pritzerber See, Kreis Westhavelland. Edged part of a reindeer antler pickaxe.

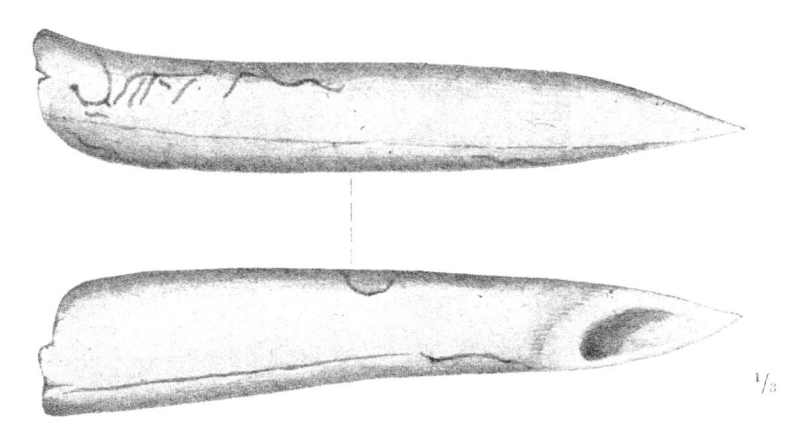

Fig. 7: Hohenferchesar, Kreis Westhavelland. Lance point made of reindeer antlers with animal carvings.

examples of Ancylus implements. Nevertheless, it is a completely groundless conjecture[1]. We still do not know of any such physical remnants from the sparse population of this early period.

Around 12,000 BC, the northeastern German coast along with Zealand and southern Sweden also became ice-free[2]. During this period, that is, during the sea

---

[1] I will soon publish more details about this in the *Mannus* journal.
[2] Sophus Müller: *Aarbøger for nordisk Oldkyndighed og Historie* 1896, pp. 304 ff.; Georg Sarauw: *Aarbøger f. n. O.* 1903, pp. 303 ff

ice stage of the Baltic Sea, the so-called Yoldia period (see the map on p. 86), when the ice had receded to the central Swedish lake basin, to the west coast of Finland, and into the interior of Norway, there were certain roughly hewn "almond-shaped" or more aptly long-oval flint tools (Fig. 9), some of considerable size, which are found on Rügen, in Denmark, in southern and western Sweden, and in southwestern Norway in what are geologically the oldest strata in Scandinavia that contain any human implements at all[1].

However, it is only the legacy of the descendants of those post-Ice-Age people from the second half of the next period of the formation of the Baltic Sea, in which it became a freshwater inland sea, and which is called its Ancylus stage, (see the map on p. 87), that can be richly attested to. This population was able to advance as far as central Sweden, southern Norway, and Finland,[2] and their skeletal remains, which in some instances in northern Germany were

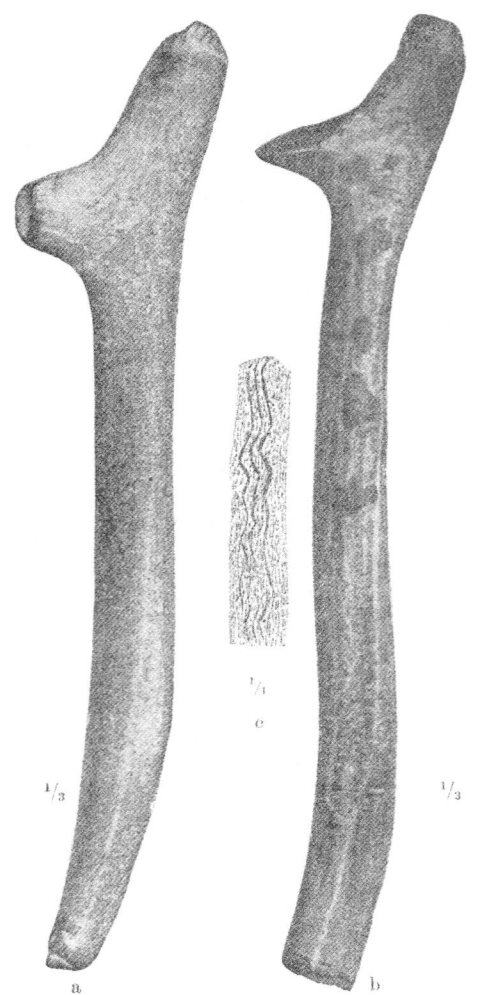

Fig. 8, a–c: Two reindeer antler shafts made into axes (a, b), one (b) decorated with a wavy band (c). a: Jutland; b, c: Funen. (*Aarb. f. n. Oldk.* 1896).

---

[1] Oscar Montelius: "De mandelförmiga flintverktygens ålder" (*Antikvarist Tidskrift för Sverige* 1919, Bd. 20, No. 6, pp. 1 ff.); see N. Niklasson: *Korrespondenz-Blatt der Deutschen Gesellschaft für Anthropologie* 1920. Bd. 51, pp. 19 ff. — Contrary to the incorrect dating of these implements to the Paleolithic Solutrean, see. Josef Bayer: "Das vermeintliche Solutréen in Skandinavien" (*Mannus* 13, 1921, pp. 1 ff.); see also Friis Johansen: *Aarbøger f. n. O.* 1919, p. 225, Footnote 3. Regarding such implements from the "Nordland" near Kristiansund in southwestern Norway see Anders Nummedal: "Nogen primitive Stenaldersformer i Norge" (*Oldtiden: Tidsskrift for norsk forhistorie* IX, Kristiania 1920, pp. 145 ff.).

[2] A most notable new find from this period is one discovered on the Vuoksi in the Antrea parish (near Viborg) in Finnish Karelia, a fishing net from deep into the Ancylus stage attached to long rows of sinking stones and net floats: Harald Lindberg in: *Öfversigt af finska Vetenskaps-societetens Förhandlingar* LVIII, 1915/16, C No. 2, pp. 19 ff. and Sakari Pälsi: "Ein steinzeitlicher Moorfund" (*Finska Fornminnesföreningens Tidskrift* 28. Helsingfors. 1920, Nos. 2 and 3 and with Fig.)

well-preserved, reveal that they belonged in a uniform fashion to both the long-headed and short-headed branches of the Western European racial strain.

Two excellently preserved long-skulls typical of the Nordic race with a broad, flat forehead and a pointed occiput were unearthed from layers of clay at Pritzerber Lake, in the district of Westhavelland, which contained bone implements from the civilization of the Ancylus period. They are in the collection of Dr. Richard Stimming in Gross-Wusterwitz near Brandenburg an der Havel, to whom I am indebted for the drawings in Figs. 10 and 11. Skull I from 1897, with a Wormian bone at the lambdoid suture, has a length of 186 and a width of 132 mm, so its cephalic index is 70.9; Skull II from 1901 has the dimensions 180:127, so a cephalic index of 70.5.

Of the numerous very ancient short peat-skulls that I previously ascribed to the Ancylus period, I would now like to solely focus on the one from Dömitz on the Elbe in

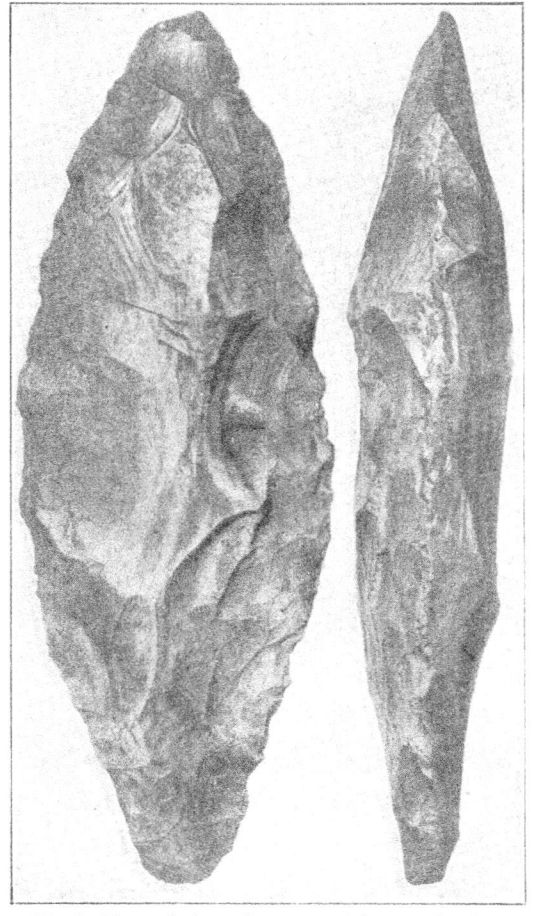

Fig. 9: Almond-shaped stone tool from Bohuslän. Approximately ⅓. (per Montelius).

Mecklenburg, and especially on the one from Spandau. The Dömitz skull, with a cephalic index of only 79.8, that is, sitting on the cusp between the long-skulls and the short-skulls (assuming one counts the medium-skull among the long-skulls, as is now customary) was dredged in 1871 from the bed of the Elbe at a depth of 20 feet below the lowest water level, in other words, as Rudolf Virchow has indicated, it was so deep that it apparently dates back to well beyond the Alluvial period[1].

---

[1] *Verhandlungen der Berliner Gesellschaft für Anthropologie* 1872, p. 7, p. 72; 1882, pp. 374 f.

The Spandau bog-skull, whose dimensions are 173:153 and whose cephalic index is 88.4, and which according to Schaaffhausen[1] is robust, roundish, with a low but broad and strongly protruding forehead, strongly protruding parietal humps, moderate eye arches, and a deeply recessed bridge of the nose, was found in 1881 at the mouth of the Spree while digging for an excavation, in which a pile-dwelling was uncovered, and between the piles the famed bronze weapon find from the end of Period II of the Bronze Age was discovered. The tips of the piles were driven into diluvial gravel and sand, over which lay loose bog silt and solid

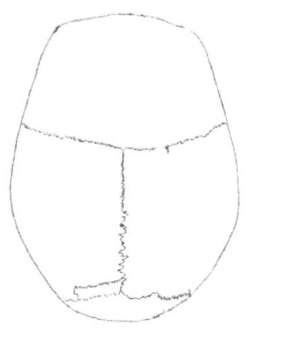

Fig. 10: ¹/₄.   Fig. 11: ¹/₄.
Pritzerber See, Kreis Westhavelland. Collection of R. Stimming, Gr. Wusterwitz.
Top views of skulls No. I and II.

peat. In the bog silt lay the bronze weapons, but also the skull, along with a bone spearhead[2] that was serrated on one side, four Type I deer antler pickaxes (shaft holes on the burr), a Type II deer antler pickaxe (shaft hole at the base of a side branch), and a small and round deer antler disc: all of these being authentic implements from the latest civilization of the Ancylus period.

With the greatest certainty, however, I would also group the grave find from Plau in Mecklenburg in this category, which in my opinion represents the oldest burial of all in the Nordic region. In 1846, a skeleton in a crouching position was uncovered about 1.80m deep in the gravelly sand without any stone protection, and alongside it were a deer antler pickaxe of Type I, two split boar tusks, and two pierced and one unpierced incisors from deer[3], in other words, there were nothing

---

[1] *Verh. d. Berl. Ges. f. Anthr.* 1882, p. 117; also see Rudolf Virchow: *ibid.* pp. 371 ff., Panel XIV, 1–4
[2] See *Archiv für Anthropologie* Bd. 14, 1883, pp. 378 ff, Panel IV, Fig. 19 (Ernst Friedel).
[3] R. Beltz: *Die vorgeschichtlichen Altertümer des Großherzogtums Mecklenburg-Schwerin.* Berlin 1910, p. 108. *Jahrbücher des Vereins für mecklenburgische Geschichte* 12, p. 400; 14, p. 301; — On the boar tusks: *Verh. d. Berl. Gel. f. Anthr.* 1888, pp. 445 f. (O. Olshausen) with Fig.; The deer antler pickaxe illustrated by R. Beltz: *Die Vorgeschichte von Mecklenburg.* Berlin 1899, p. 8, Fig. 5 and Beltz: *Die vorgeschichtlichen Altertümer des Großherzogtums Mecklenburg-Schwerin.* Table 15, Fig. 137.

but bone implements, while stone implements were completely absent. The skull[1] of the skeleton (Fig. 12), a genuine roundhead with a cephalic index of 86.36, looks extraordinarily archaic due to its coarse, massive structure, thickness of the skull bones, recessed forehead, imposing arched brow ridge, perfectly steep yet wide, low face, and the vertical extension of the wide, stout lower jaw lacking genuine protrusion of the chin (which is otherwise noted only in the Neanderthal race). According to Schliz, who erroneously considers this to be a Late Neolithic grave, this skull can be equated with the Swedish short-skulls of the Karleby woman and those of Hällekis[2], whose progenitor it therefore must have been.

Fig. 12: Plau in Mecklenburg.

We thus have attested to two long-skulls and 1–3 short-skulls of the people of the Ancylus period. As fishers and hunters, this people had their raft-dwellings exclusively on lakes and standing bodies of water until the end of the Ancylus stage. No exception to this were some of the Swedish dwelling-places from this time, which were located on what was then the shore of the Baltic Sea, since at the time it also was still a true inland sea.

---

[1] Pictured: *Jahrb. f. meckl. Gesch.* 1859, 24, p. 188 (Schaafhausen) and *Archiv für Anthropologie* N. S. VII. 1908, pp. 276 ff. Fig. 1 (Schliz).
[2] Retzius: *Crania suecica antiqua.* Stockholm 1900. Nr. 21 and 32.

— 18 —

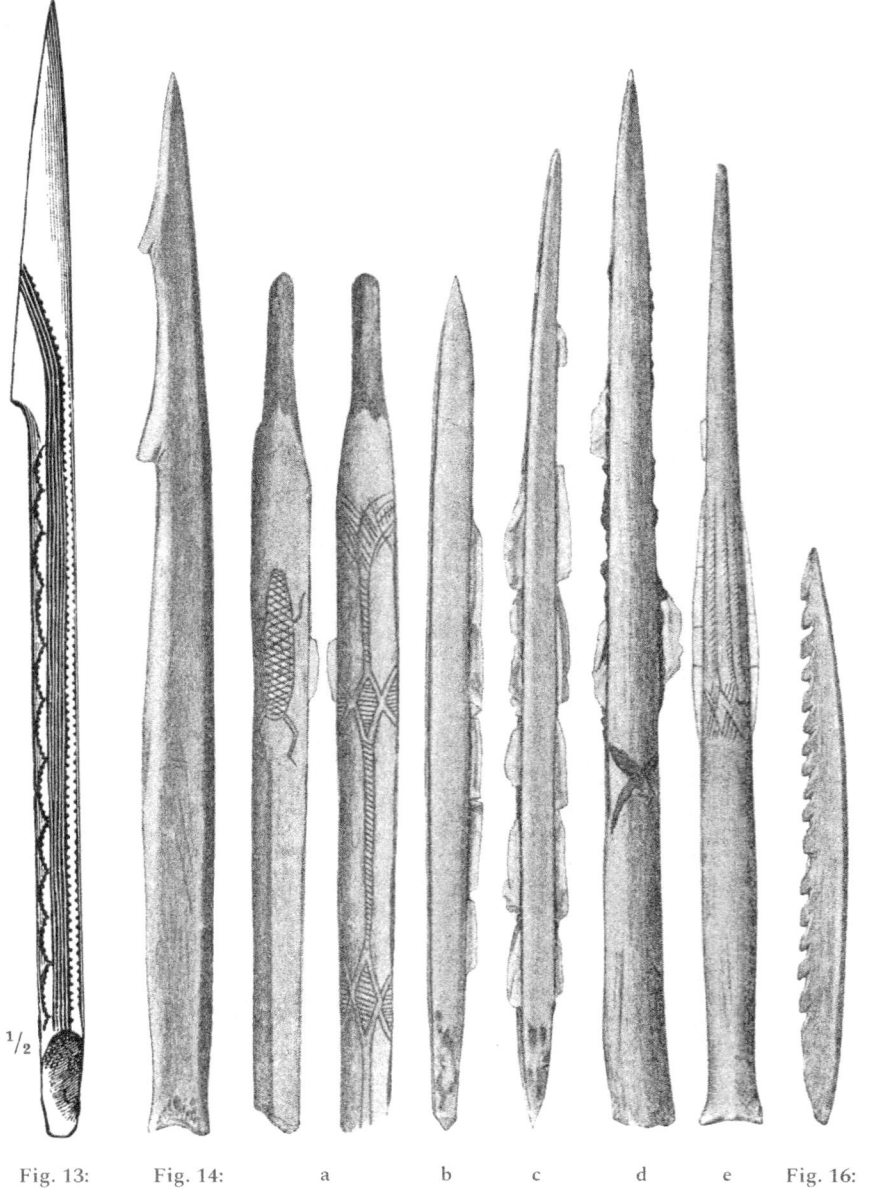

Fig. 13: Peitschendorf, Kreis Sensburg, East Prussia. Bone point with resin inlay. Museum Königsberg.

Fig. 14: ¹/₂. Bone point. Denmark.

Fig. 15: ¹/₂. Bone points with flint blades. Denmark (per A.P. Madsen).
a b c d e

Fig. 16: Finely serrated bone point. Denmark (per Madsen).

Fig. 17: Fish harpoon. Gr. Kreuz, Kreis Zauch-Belzig. Märkisches Museum Berlin.

— 19 —

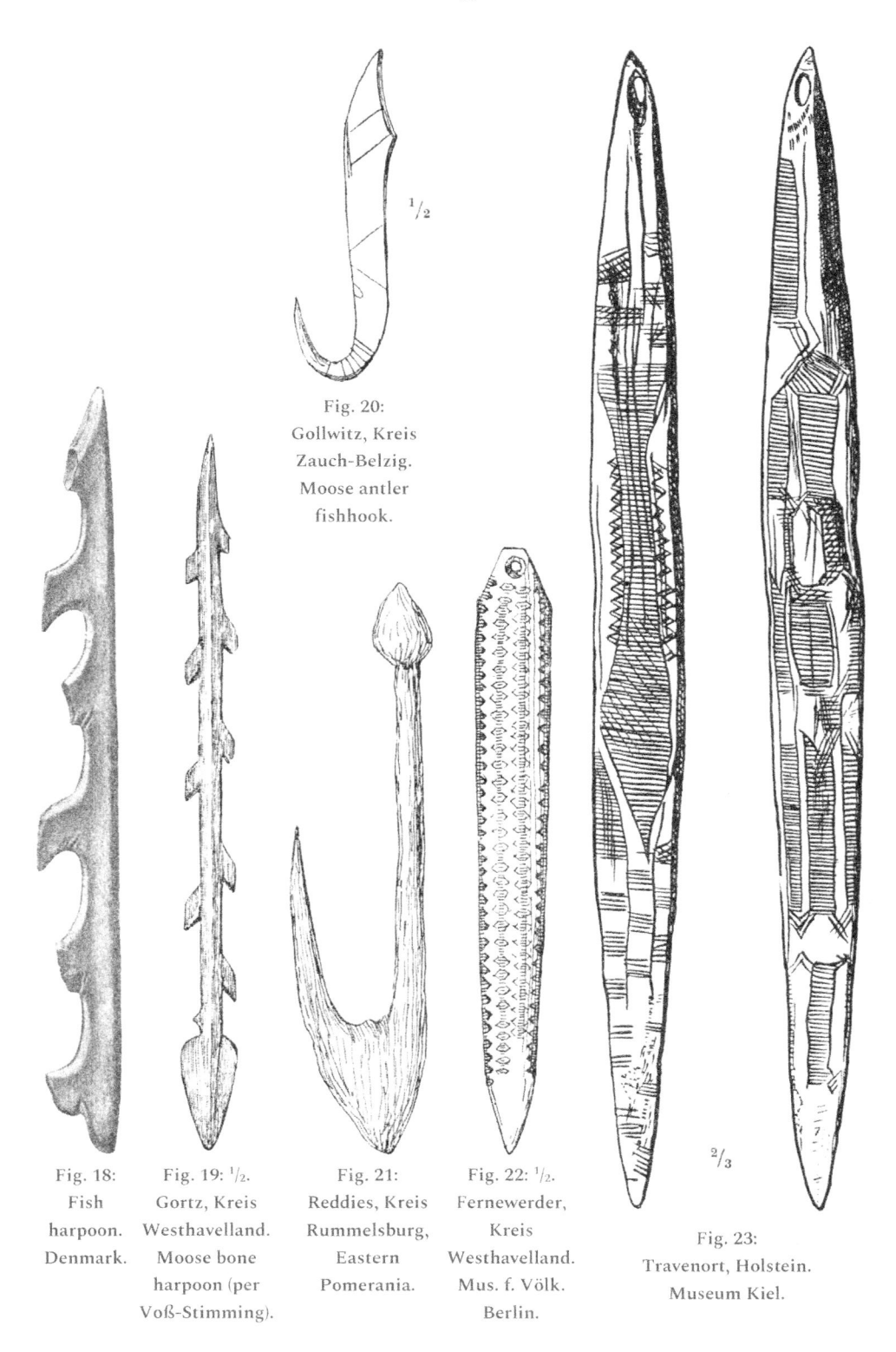

Fig. 20: Gollwitz, Kreis Zauch-Belzig. Moose antler fishhook.

Fig. 18: Fish harpoon. Denmark.

Fig. 19: ¹/₂. Gortz, Kreis Westhavelland. Moose bone harpoon (per Voß-Stimming).

Fig. 21: Reddies, Kreis Rummelsburg, Eastern Pomerania.

Fig. 22: ¹/₂. Fernewerder, Kreis Westhavelland. Mus. f. Völk. Berlin.

Fig. 23: Travenort, Holstein. Museum Kiel.

I call this population the Dobbertin people after the earliest find from Dobbertin[1] near Goldberg in Mecklenburg, which was discovered in 1866 and was correctly scientifically assessed straightaway; in Denmark, the find site of *Maglemose* near Mullerup on Zealand has more recently become another namesake for this population[2].

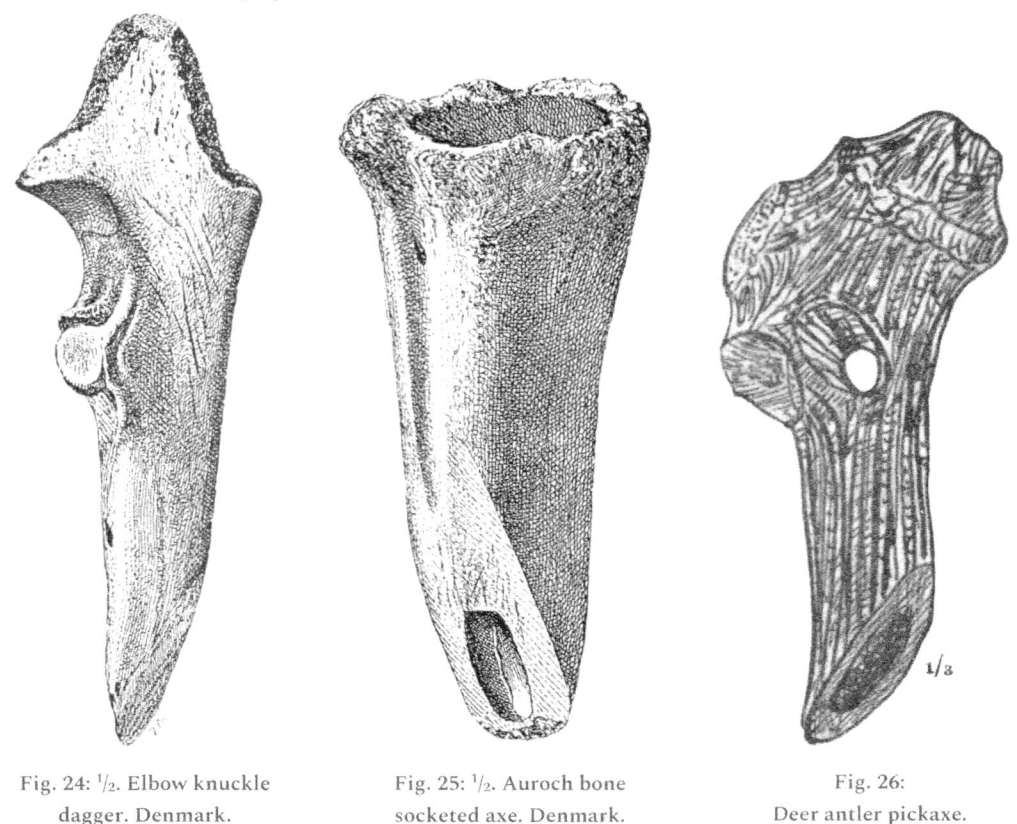

Fig. 24: ¹/₂. Elbow knuckle dagger. Denmark.

Fig. 25: ¹/₂. Auroch bone socketed axe. Denmark.

Fig. 26: Deer antler pickaxe.

In the design of their implements, the Dobbertiners often show even closer ties to the artifacts of the post-Ice-Age Magdalenian period, and likewise in their ability and habit of decorating these implements with naturalistic animal drawings or geometric patterns (Figs. 13, 15a, 22, 23, 27, 28; compare with Figs. 6c, 7).

Implements that were particularly characteristic of their way of life[3] were

---

[1] Friedrich Lisch: *Jahrb. d. Ver. f. meckl. Geschichte* Bd. 34, 1869, pp. 210 ff.
[2] Georg Sarauw: *Aarbøger f. n. O.* 1903, pp. 148 ff.
[3] Latest representation of this civilization by K. Friis Johansen: "En Boplads fra den äldste Stenalder i Svärdborg Mose" (*Aarbøger f. nord. Oldk.* 1919, pp. 106 ff. = *Mémoires de la Société des Antiquaires du Nord* 1918-19, pp. 241 ff.).

hunting weapons and fishing implements made from the bones and antlers of moose, deer, and aurochs. These included bone points that are either completely smooth (Fig. 13) or that had one or a few small straight barbs on just one side (Fig. 14), partly with use of flint inserts in two longitudinal grooves on the side (so-called "bird-arrows") (Fig. 15 a–e), which formed the front end of throwing lances[1], also fish hooks (Figs. 20, 21), "net lifters" (also called "smoothers") (Figs. 22, 23), tools for net weaving, daggers made from elbow bones (Fig. 24), socketed axes made from long bones of aurochs (Fig. 25), chisels made from antlers (see Fig. 39g), and shaft hole pickaxes made from the root end (burr portion) of deer antlers (Figs. 26–28). A somewhat later phase of the same period, which can be dated to

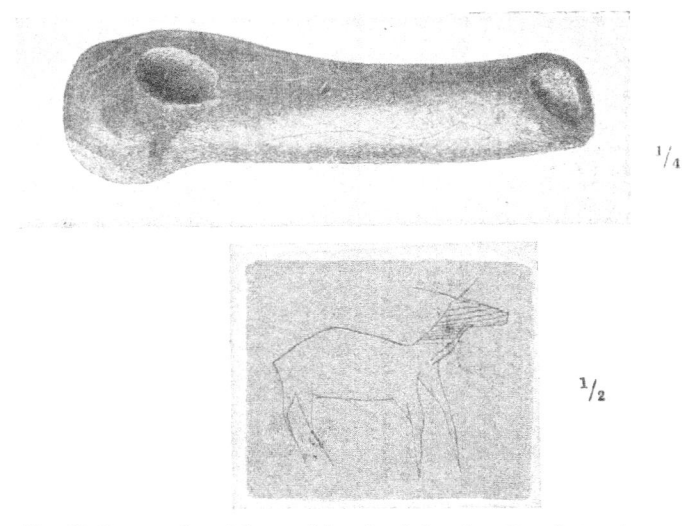

Fig. 27: Deer antler pickaxe with animal drawing. Ystad, Scania.

around 7000 BC, is represented by bone points that have fine densely perforated teeth along one side (Fig. 16). Later still are the crude, heavy harpoons, with many large, strongly curved barbs along one or both sides, and with a protuberance or hole at the end of the handle for attaching the line: implements (Figs. 17, 18, 19) which, like the bone points with flint edges, persisted during the Shell Midden period as one of the inheritances from the days of the Ancylus period, although they did not appear all that often. In northern Germany these later specimens were still carved from the shovels of moose antlers; in Denmark, on the other hand, when the moose vanished as a result of the extinction of the conifers at the end of the Ancylus period, they were primarily carved from the antlers of roe deer.

---

[1] Once, in a peat bog at Esperöd, Tranås parish in Scania, a bone lance point was found connected to the skeleton of a pike (*Ymer*. Stockholm 1917, p. 453).

Flint was also used extensively by the Dobbertiners, but in far less elaborate forms; embryonic core axes (Figs. 29–31) and embryonic cleavers are found in rare instances, while points (Fig. 32), round scrapers (Fig. 33), and disk scrapers (Fig. 34) are common finds. Characteristic here is the predominance of quite tiny, very reliably and skillfully crafted so-called microlithic implements[1], mostly triangular

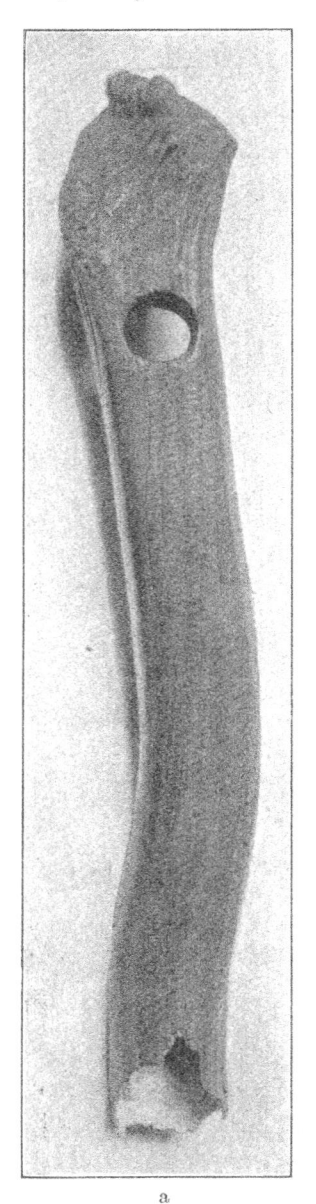

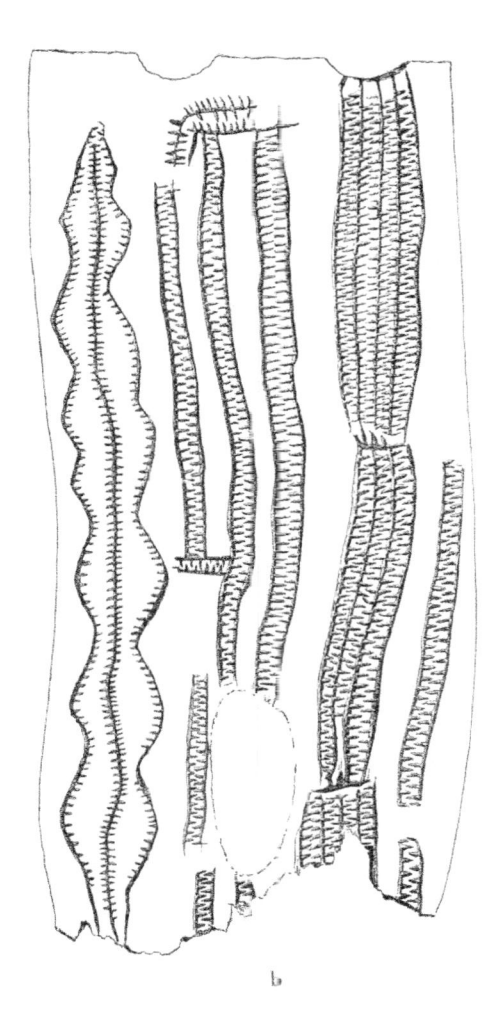

Fig. 28: a, b. ³/₈. Deer antler pickaxe (a) with rich decoration in resin inlay (b: unfurled depiction). Kleinmachnow near Berlin.

---

[1] Sarauw: *Prähistorische Zeitschrift* V, 1914, pp. 7 ff. and Friis Johansen: *Mémoires de la Société des Antiquaires du Nord* 1918–19, pp. 268 ff.

in shape and occasionally with an arched shape, which found use partly as arrowheads and partly as barbs which were embedded in various quantities on one side of a wooden lance point[1]. These microlithics, which also had counterparts among the Western European Azilian-Tardenoisian cultures (Fig. 35), could still be found from the beginning of the

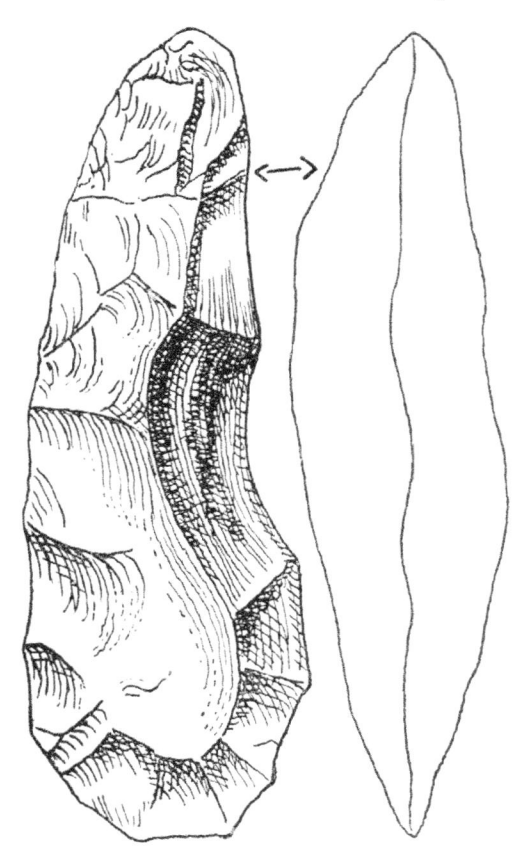

Fig. 29: Core axe: Frontal and lateral views.

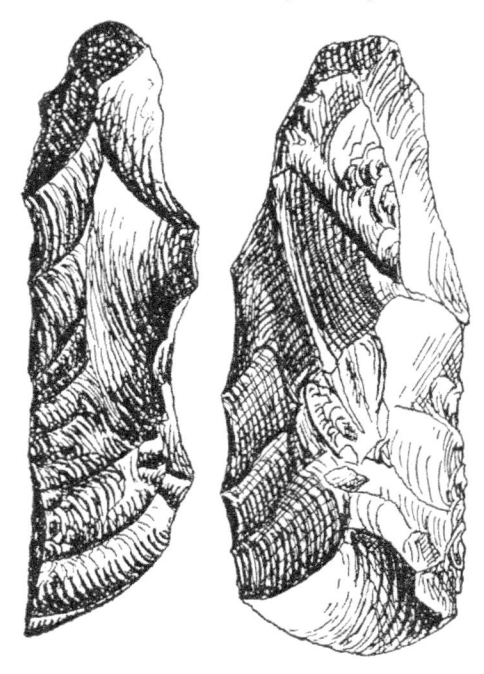

Fig. 30: Transverse axe (pickaxe): Frontal and lateral views.

Kalbe an der Milde, Altmark (per *Zeitschrift für Ethnologie* 1907).

next period, the Shell Midden period, after which they disappear from the record.

Of particular relevance is the fact is that among these flint, bone, and antler striking tools we find only transverse axes, transverse pickaxes, and chisels (where the cutting edge is transverse to the direction of the shaft), but never straight axes

---

[1] Quite remarkable is the discovery in 1906 of a complete auroch skeleton from the peat at Jyderup near Vig in Odsherred on Zealand, in whose chest three microlithic arrowheads characteristic of the Ancylus period were found. The badly wounded bull, whose 7th rib had healed and whose 9th rib shows an unhealed wound, in which the remnants of a flint arrowhead are still stuck, had apparently gone to a nearby pond to relieve his pain, but had died in it (N. Hartz and H. Winge: *Aarbøger f. n. O.* 1908, pp. 225 ff.).

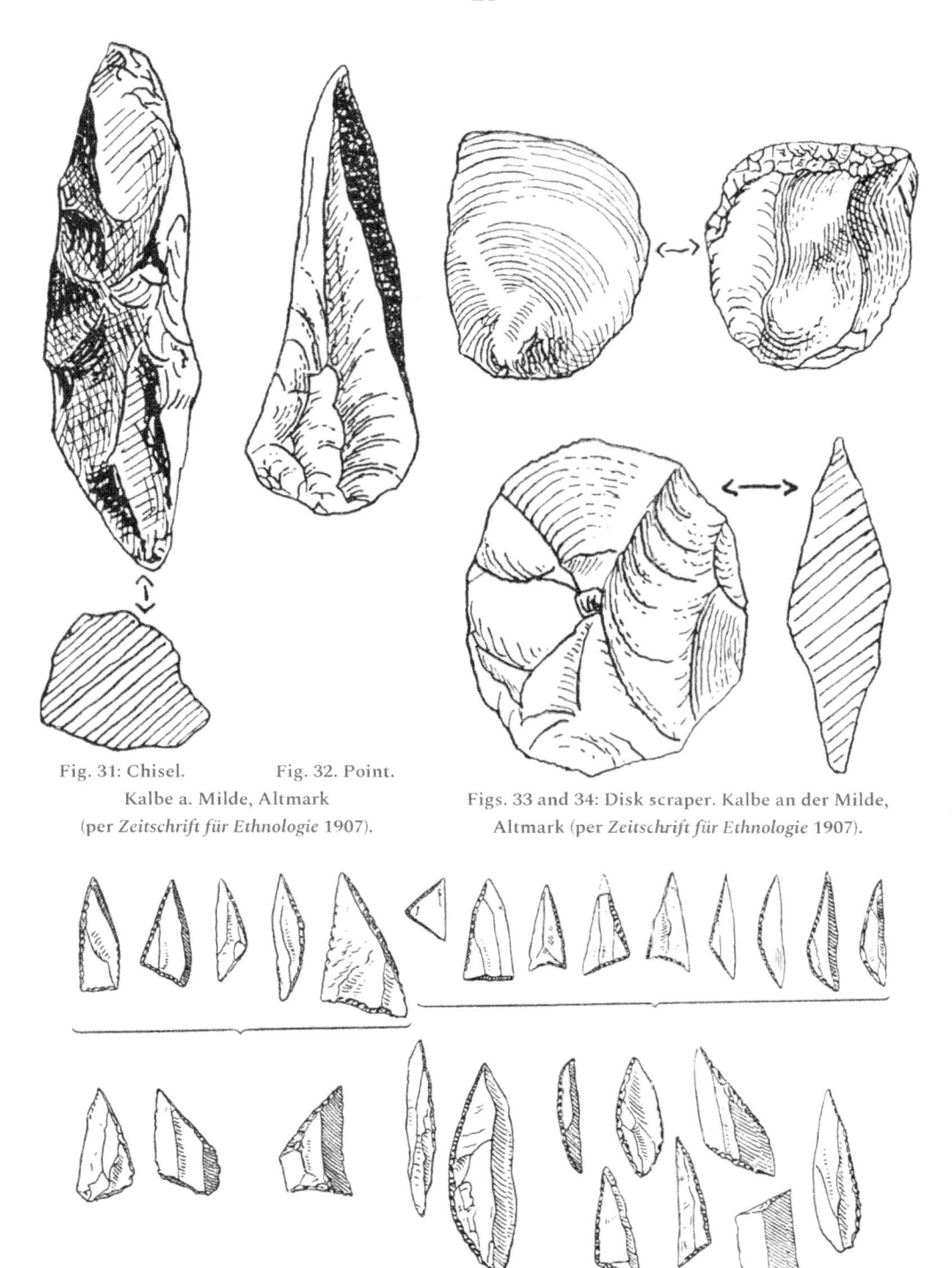

Fig. 31: Chisel.   Fig. 32. Point.
Kalbe a. Milde, Altmark
(per *Zeitschrift für Ethnologie* 1907).

Figs. 33 and 34: Disk scraper. Kalbe an der Milde, Altmark (per *Zeitschrift für Ethnologie* 1907).

Fig. 35: Microlithic flint implements of the European Tardenoisians (per M. Hörnes): triangular, arched, trapezoidal, or rhombus-shaped.

(where the cutting edge is parallel to the direction of the shaft). This characteristic which is reflective of a primitive civilization connects the Dobbertiners of the

Fig. 36: Baltic Sea Region in the Littorina Stage. The dashed arc lines (isobases) connect the points of equal elevation; the numbers indicate how much higher (in meters) the land and sea floor are today than during the time of the Littorina.

Ancylus period with their descendants of the Arctic civilization of the Later Stone Age in Scandinavia, Finland, and Russia (and also with the Eskimos), whereas the Pre-Indo-Germanics of the Shell Midden period were already familiar with the straight axe in addition to the transverse axe and the pickaxe.

The language of these people can only have been the further developed Western European language of the post-Ice-Age: certainly still agglutinative, that is, the relationships of the words in the sentence are expressed by prefixes, suffixes, and infixes, not by inflection. The aforementioned later stage of this civilization from the end of the Ancylus stage, whose principal characteristic was the fine-toothed bone point (Fig. 16), has its characteristic and eponymous find sites at Kunda in Estonia[1] and at Viste[2] in Jæderen in southern Norway. M. Olsen[3]

Fig. 37: Grave of skeleton from the shell midden near Aamølle, Jutland.

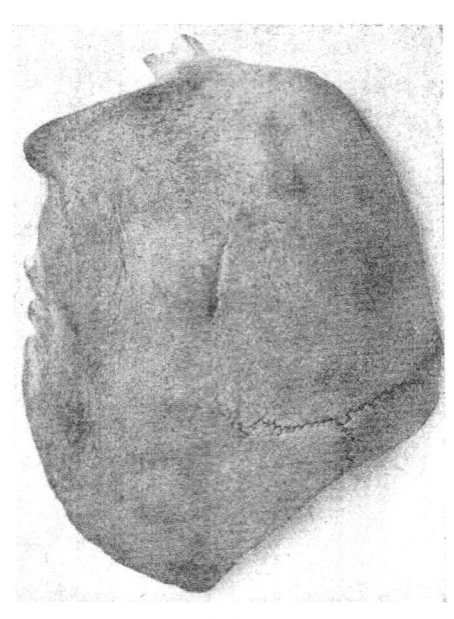

Fig. 38: Kiel-Ellerbek. Museum Kiel K. S. 11245b. Top of frontal process.

has identified the word *viste*, which in Norway occurs eight times as a homestead name (northward only as far as Trondheim), used at times for groups of farms or homesteads, as the name that the Indo-Germanics (most probably already Germanics) who moved here several thousand years later used to designate these ancient dwelling-places which had belonged to an extinct population of fishers. The Lappish *vista* means "dwelling house" and is an Indo-Germanic or Germanic

---

[1] Grewingk: "Geologie und Archäologie des Mergellagers von Kunda in Esthland." Dorpat 1882 (*Archiv für die Naturkunde Liv-, Ehst- und Kurlands*, Series I. Bd. IX, 1); Grewingk: "Die neolithischen Bewohner von Kunda in Esthland" (*Verhandlungen der Gelehrten Estnischen Gesellschaft zu Dorpat* 1884).

[2] A. W. Brögger: Vistefundet. Stavanger 1908; A. W. Brögger: "Vistefundet" (*Naturen*, November 1910, pp. 332 ff.); Carl M. Fürst: *Das Skelett von Viste auf Jäderen, ein Fall von Staphocephalie*. Christiania 1909. — [See Supplements on p. 82].

[3] M. Olsen: "Stedsnavne og arkaeologi" (*Oldtiden*, Rygh-Festskriftet 1914, pp. 116 ff.).

loanword[1].

Around 6000 B.C., a predominantly long-headed population broke away from this mixed long-headed and short-headed inland population of Dobbertiners in order to settle on the coasts and islands of the Baltic Sea, which by then, as a result of a new stage in its formation, had again become an unenclosed saltwater sea (Littorina stage of the Baltic Sea: Fig. 36).

Of the human skeletons recovered from the Danish shell middens (see Fig. 37), two have proved to have long-skulls, a male from Fannerup in Jutland with a cephalic index of 76.9, and a female from Holbæk on Zealand with a cephalic index of 74.2, which are contrasted only by a male skeleton from Kassemose on Zealand, which has a skull typical of the Grenelle type with a cephalic index of 82[2]. The Ellerbek site has yielded a number of skullcaps, which unfortunately were all incompletely preserved, but insofar as there is a conclusion that can be drawn here, they indicate that we are dealing with long-skulls, which, when compared to later ones, possess very archaic features, but of such a kind that, according to Fürst, is also seen among some Swedish Stone Age skulls (Fig. 38). An expert examination and analysis of these skulls is an urgent scientific necessity[3]. Through friendly correspondence with Dr. Med. Jens Paulsen in Kiel, I have learned that these skulls are characterized by strikingly thick bone walls reminiscent of Paleolithic forms (up to 10 mm thick), and in some cases also by a strongly projecting brow, a receding forehead, and a ridge-like elevation of the frontal suture.

According to a racial-psychological law, the longheads within a racial strain always form the enterprising, adventurous, wanderlusting, conquering, but at the same time also creative, inventive, progress-oriented, and thereby aristocratic-ideal-directed part of the population, while the shortheads, on the other hand, form the tenaciously entrenched and stubbornly preservation-oriented part of the population, which is averse to progress, adventure, and warlike wandering, is politically democratic, and is concerned only with its own advantage.

Whilst the Dobbertin population was settling to the south of the Baltic Sea in

---

[1] Wiklund: *Le Monde Oriental* 1911, p. 236.

[2] H. A. Nielsen: *Aarbøger f. nord. Oldk.* 1911, p. 90, No. 91 (Fannerup); p. 112, No. 370 (Holbæk); p. 100, No. 238 (Kassemose).

[3] Recently, in Sweden, and in an inversion of a view I have long espoused, it has been suggested that the Dobbertin people had belonged to a purely long-skulled race, and that, with the Ellerbekers, a people of a purely short-skulled race had grafted itself upon them — this is to turn established fact on its head.

the region of eastern Hanover and Schleswig-Holstein and further eastward through Mecklenburg, Brandenburg, Pomerania, and Posen on into Estonia, and was primarily concentrated in the east, that is, in northeastern Germany and also in Denmark on the islands (yet not on Jutland), we then encounter a new coastal

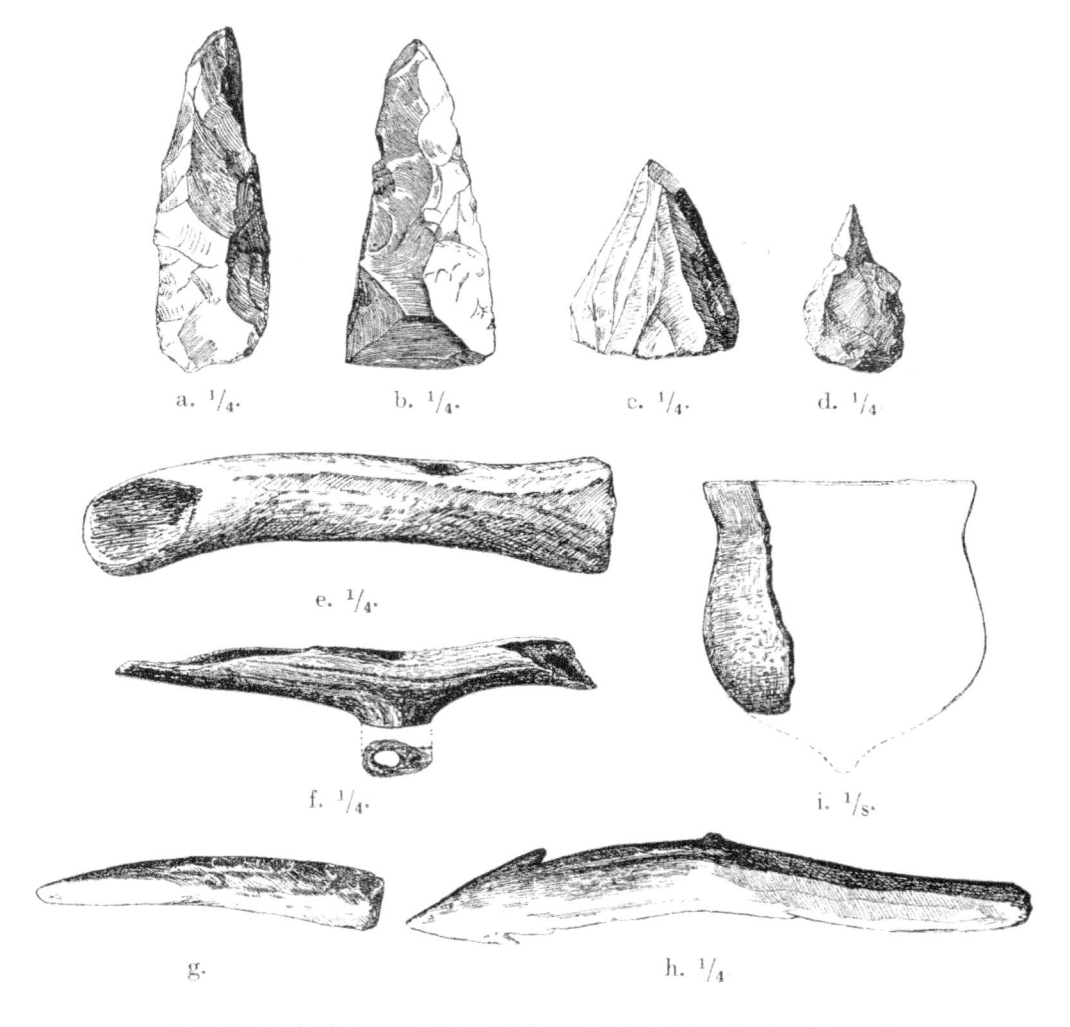

Fig. 39 a–i: Ellerbek near Kiel. Finds from the Early Littorina (per Mestorf).

population south of the Baltic Sea that was located primarily in the west: in Western Pomerania, on Rügen, on the east coasts of Schleswig-Holstein and Jutland, and, just as with the former population, also on the Danish islands and on the Swedish west coast. I call this coastal population the "Ellerbek people" after the most important and especially ancient site of Ellerbek in the Port of

Kiel[1]; in Denmark they have also recently been named after the ancient shell middens of Ertebölle on the Limfjord[2]. While the Dobbertiners made their most characteristic civilizational tools and weapons from bone and antler, the Ellerbekers poured all of their energy into the development of flint technology, which the Dobbertiners also used extensively, but with craftsmanship that was far less intricate. The Ellerbekers created exquisite flint weapons and implements in a greater variety of forms, predominantly straight axes, by developing the even smaller core axe (Fig. 29) and the imperfect cleaving axe, which had been inherited from the Dobbertiners, to

Fig. 40: ²/₃. Petersfehner Moor in Oldenburg. Museum Oldenburg (per J. Martin). Arrow shaft with a transverse flint arrowhead and animal sinew binding.

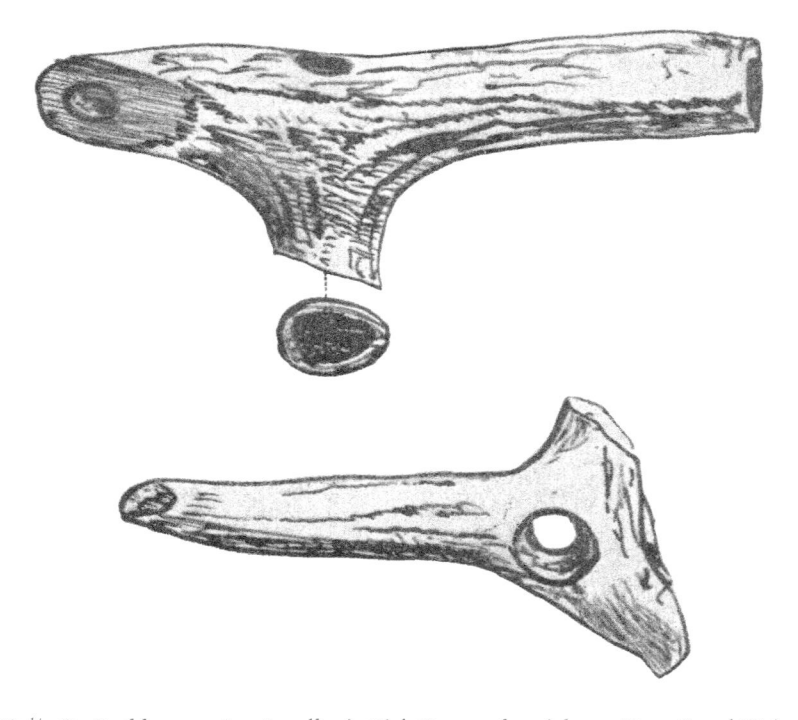

Figs. 41, 42: ¹/₃. On Bothkamper See, Landkreis Kiel. Deer antler pickaxes Type II and III (per Mestorf).

the utmost state of perfection (Fig. 39a, b). We also observe flint boring and coring tools (Fig. 39d, c). The microlithics were soon superseded by the transverse or

---

[1] J. Mestorf: *43. Bericht des Schleswig-Holsteinischen Museums vaterländischer Altertümer*. Kiel 1904.
[2] A. P. Madsen, S. Müller, et al.: *Affaldsdynger fra stenaldern i Danmark*. Copenhagen 1900.

chisel-ended flint arrowhead (Fig. 40)[1]. In addition to the older deer antler pickaxes with a shaft hole in the burr part (Fig. 39e), a new kind appeared, for which a higher segment of the antler from the point where the extension of a side branch begins was used (Fig. 39f). Vestiges of the Ancylus period that made an appearance include antler chisels (Fig. 39g) and a broad, flat point made of barbed deer antlers (Fig. 39h). In addition, the Ellerbekers were learning the basics of the craft of pottery-making; this was characterized by large clay jugs with pointed bases: Figs. 39i and 43. Towards the end of the period of the earlier shell middens, similar vessels appeared which, due to a subtler tapering of what was previously only an S-shaped curved wall, already demonstrated a division of the vessel body into neck and belly, and which were also already decorated with two rows of indented lines under the rim (Fig. 44) or with clusters of vertical cord impressions on the upper part of the belly (Fig. 45).

Fig. 43: ¹/₆. Brabrand Lake, Ning Herred, Jutland. (per *Aarböger* 1906).

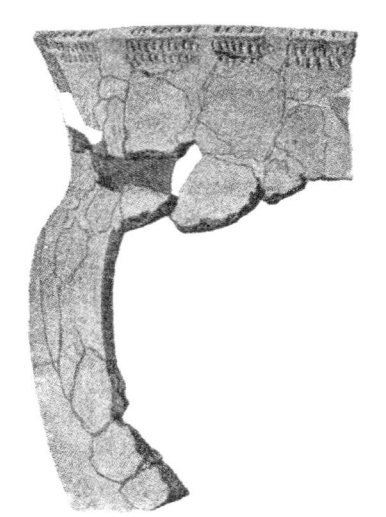

Figs. 44, 45: ¹/₄. Sølager shell midden near Roskilde, Zealand.

---

[1] Although this type of arrowhead is found in large numbers among the Ellerbekers (among the Dobbertiners it only sporadically appears at the end of the Ancylus period), it is extremely rare for complete arrows with wooden shafts to have been preserved. In addition to the Oldenburg piece (J. Martin: *Jahrb. f. d. Gesch. D. Herz.* Oldenburg. 1880, p. 588), there is also one from a peat bog near Tellingstedt in North Dithmarschen (*Katalog der Ausstellung prähistorischer und anthropologischer Funde Deutschlands zu Berlin*. 1880, S. 588), and two from peat bog finds in Denmark (A. P. Madsen: *Afbildninger Af Danske Oldsager Og Mindesmærker: Stenalderen*. Copenhagen 1868, p. 24, Plate 22, Figs. 18, 19 from Odense on Funen; *Aarbøger f. n. Oldk.* 1917 from Ejsing parish, Ginding Herred in North Jutland).

The Ellerbekers thus became a people unto themselves and must have also progressed their language more rapidly than the stubbornly entrenched Dobbertiners. It is them that I see as the Pre-Indo-Germanics.

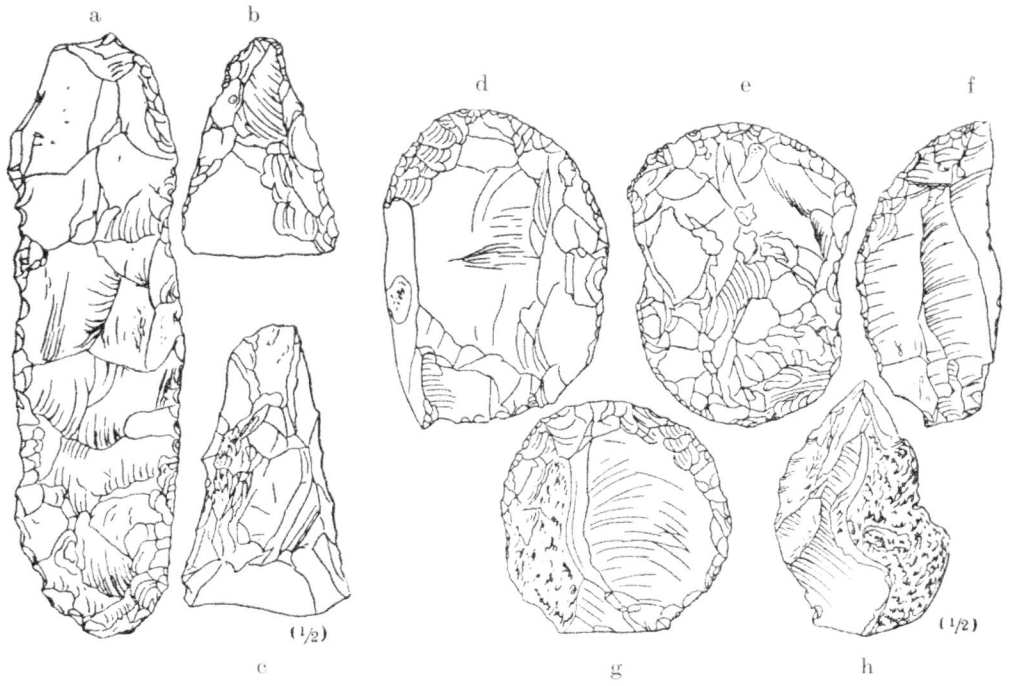

Fig. 46: Flint implements of the northern French/Belgian Campignian culture. a) core axe; b,c) cleaving axe; d,e,g) round scraper and spoon scraper, f) chipping knife in the shape of a parrot's beak and h) borer.

Fig. 47: ¹/₄. Forsinge, Jutland.   Fig. 48: ¹/₄. Bornholm.   Fig. 49: ¹/₄. Bornholm.

Vigorous proliferation coupled with a desire for conquest drove large segments of the Ellerbekers to the west, whitherto they flowed through Belgium and northeastern France into a broad wedge-shaped settlement area which stretched as far southwestwards as the Dordogne (see the map on p. 88), whereupon they transplanted the Nordic civilization, which became known as the Campignian culture (Fig. 46). They also took possession of southeastern England (see the map

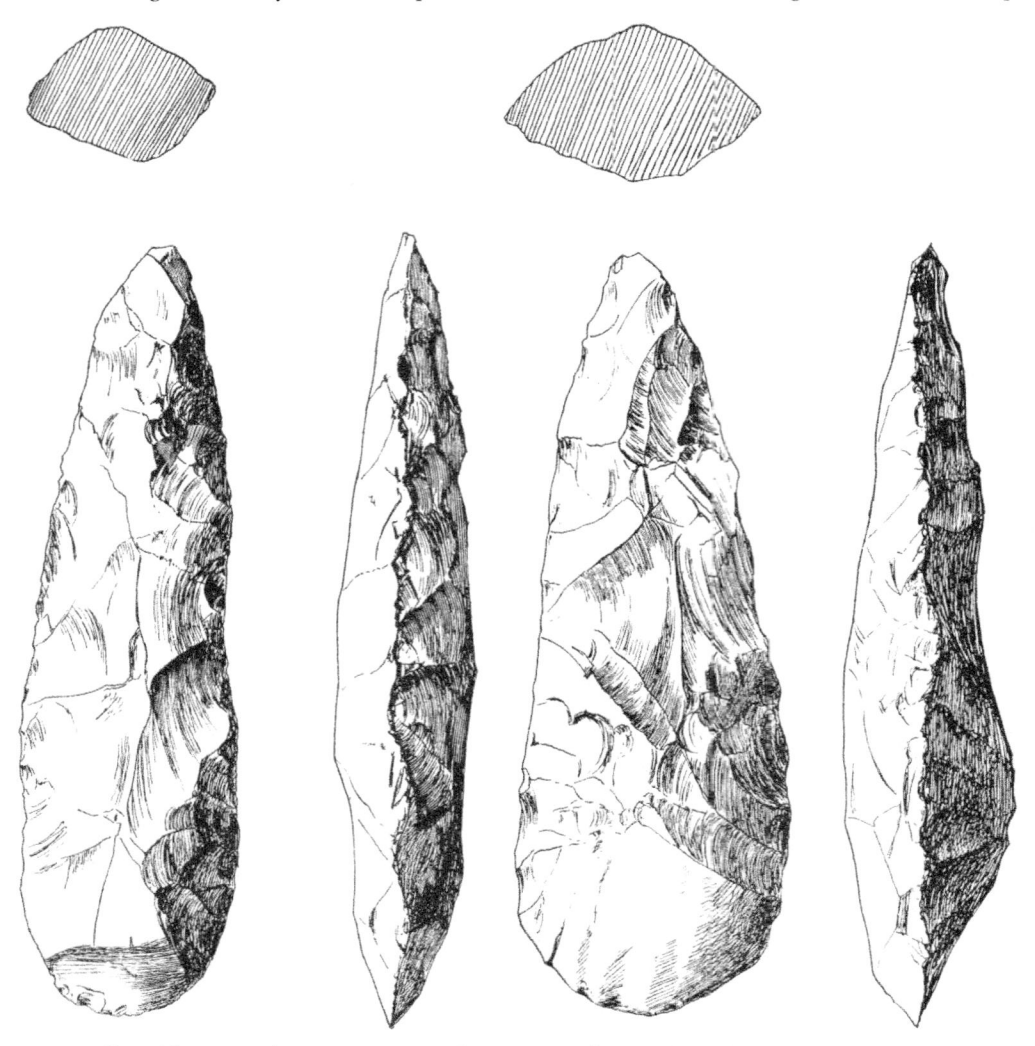

Fig. 50: ²/₃. Schleswig-Holstein. Museum Kiel. F. S. 1026. Transition from the Littorina core axe to the point-butted flint axe: on average very thick, i.e. broad sides still strongly curved; greatest width in the middle; long oval cutting edge.

Fig 51: ²/₃. Angeln, Schleswig. Mus. Kiel. K. S. 2405. Point-butted flint axe of the earliest type; broad sides still strongly curved; cutting edge still oval; but greatest width no longer in the middle, as with the earlier core axe, but already to the rear of the cutting edge. — I owe the illustrations for Figs. 50 and 51 to the Museum vat. Alt. in Kiel.

on p. 89). Both colonial areas survived until the end of the Stone Age, although flint technology here, in contrast to the area of the Baltic Sea homeland, where it continued to flourish, soon declined and eventually completely degenerated[1]. It is highly noteworthy that the area of the flint civilization in both France and Great Britain was completely distinct from the areas of those civilizations that used only solid rock as a raw material for the manufacture of axe blades. As matters stand, this distinction did not depend on the natural occurrence of the raw material. It is equally noteworthy that the areas of flint technology in both of the aforementioned countries were completely distinct from the areas of the stone tombs (see the map on p. 90). Outside of northern Germany, Central Europe remained practically unpopulated during the time of the Ellerbek civilization since the still cool, moist climate continued to favor a complete cover of primeval forest. On the other hand, we find very early representations of the two Ellerbek flint axe types, which owing to their rudimentary forms possibly date back to the Ancylus period, in southern Lithuania, southern Poland, and Volhynia (7th millennium BC)[2]. If one were to postulate that the population of these eastern colonies had promptly migrated further southeast until they reached Mesopotamia, then they could have constituted the founding stock of the Sumerians, who, according to H. Hein[3], bore a relation to the Indo-Germanics. A particularly close relationship between the Sumerians and the Greeks, as Hein assumes, is inconceivable at such an early date. On the other hand, it is in remarkable concordance with the archaeological circumstances that the Sumerian language also exhibits a closer relationship with Finno-Ugric.

In the second half of the 5th millennium, during the time of the later Danish shell middens, which were no longer close to the seashore like the earlier ones, the Ellerbek people made enormous progress in agriculture and livestock breeding[4], as well as with pottery that was closely related in both form and ornamentation to the earlier iterations, but which was more refined[5]. These later vessels are linked to the earlier type by their initially still vertically impressed

---

[1] Nils Åberg: *Studier öfver den yngre Stenåldern i Norden och Västeuropa*. Norrköping 1912. — Kossinna: *Mannus* 11/12, pp. 255 ff.
[2] *Światowit*, Vol. III. Warsaw, 1911. Plate IV; Vol. IV. 1902, pp. 97 ff, Figs. 18, 42, 59, 64; Vol. V. 1904. — Nils Åberg: *Das nordische Kulturgebiet in Mitteleuropa während der jüngeren Steinzeit*. Uppsala 1918. I, p. 3.
[3] *Mannus* 11/12, 1919, pp. 181 ff.
[4] At the Limhamn settlement near Malmö, where not the slightest trace of a piece of polished flint has been found, a potsherd with an impression of a wheat grain and several other sherds with impressions of wheat and straw, as well as bones of domestic sheep, and perhaps also of domestic pig and domestic cattle, were discovered in the uppermost layers: this settlement belongs to the end of the Littorina period (the Ellerbek age) (Kjellmark: *Antiqvarist Tidskrift för Sverige*. Vol. 17, No. 3, p. 101. Stockholm 1903).
[5] S. Müller: *Stenalderens Kunst i Danmark*. Copenhagen. 1917. — Further details: *Mannus* 13. 1921.

clusters of cord impressions, but they emphasized even more strongly the division of the structure into neck and belly. Soon, however, the clusters of vertical cord impressions transform into a band of multiple horizontally impressed cord lines which run just under the rim of the vessel (Figs. 47 to 49). One of these vessels, which I have called the "proto-Beaker," was found in a shallow earth grave; the period these vessels belong to falls before the beginnings of the large stone tombs during the period of the point-butted flint axe. This form of axe slowly developed from the core axe and was initially simply hewn, but soon became well-honed (Figs. 50, 51). Around the same time, there must have also been a leap in the development of the language, which was now transitioning from the Pre-Indo-Germanic stage into a fully developed, purely inflected Indo-Germanic.

One could speculate that during the time of the transition from the earlier to the later shell middens, a branch of the Nordic Pre-Indo-Germanic population

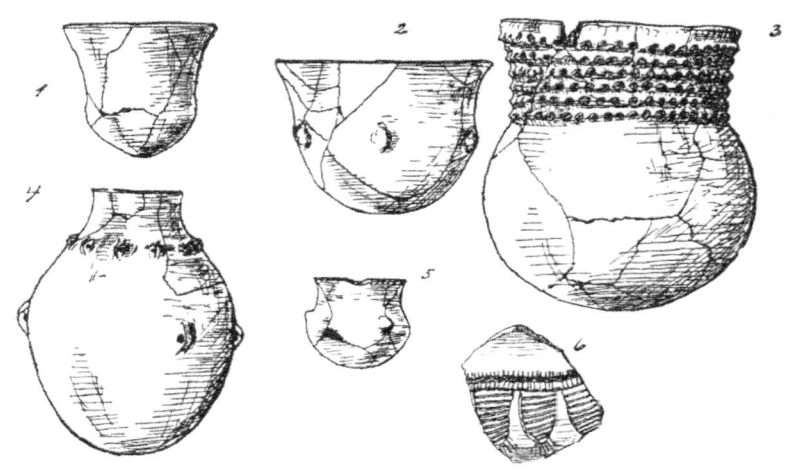

Fig. 52: Urmitz, Kreis Koblenz. Pile-dweller pottery (per A. Günther, *Mannus* II).

had migrated to the Rhine area, where stretching from Lake Constance down to Cologne we find the civilization of the land pile-dwellers which was characterized by well-made ceramic vessels, albeit ones that remained ossified in a curiously primitive form (with a rounded or pointed base, like those of the Ellerbek people: Fig. 52) that was still characteristic of the later periods of the Stone Age. This population would have then moved up into the foothills of the Alps, where they built the lake pile-dwellings, the distribution of which largely corresponds to that which linguistics has revealed about the Proto-Ligurians (place names[1] with the endings -*asco*, -*isco*). However, the pear-shaped skull of the pile-dwellers seems to

---

[1] See Ernest Muret: *Romania* XXXVII, especially p. 569.

contradict such a presumption, and according to K. F. Wolff instead reflects a derivation from the Eastern European long-headed Ryazan type.

We shall not neglect to mention here, however, that more recently the Rhenish pile dwellers have tended to be portrayed as having migrated in the opposite direction, that is, having advanced northward along the Rhine from an already Early Neolithic or even post-Ice-Age settlement hearth in Switzerland, whereby any purported connection with the Proto-Indo-Germanics would have to be abandoned.

Fig. 53: $^1/_2$. Littorina core axe, Jutland.

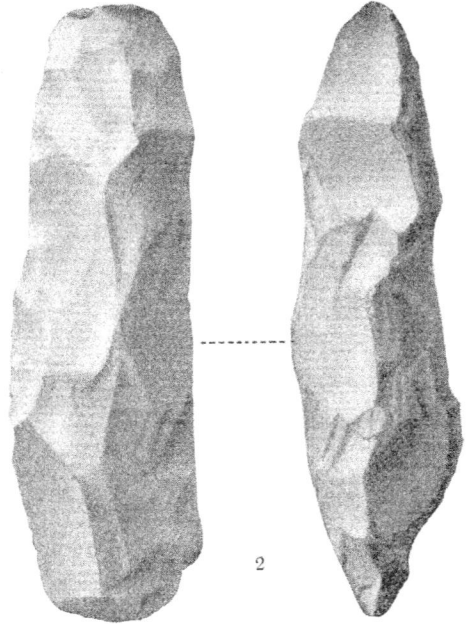

Fig. 54: $^1/_2$. Both sides of a vaulted incipient Nøstvet-Lihult axe. Smaalenene, Norway.

Figs. 53–56: per A. W. Brögger.

2. The Emergence of the Pre-Finns and Their Retreat from the Indo-Germanics

Outside of the area of the advanced Ellerbek civilization, that is, in northeastern Germany and in Scandinavia north of Bohuslän on the west coast, and on the east coast north of Blekinge, the civilization of the Dobbertin stage continued to develop along with its population, where it was primarily characterized by the Lihult Axe (Lihult in Bohuslän), which was developed under the influence of the Ellerbeker flint core axe (Fig. 53), and which in neighboring Norway is also called the Nøstvet Axe (Nøstvet near Kristiania). This axe was not made from flint, but rather from solid igneous rock, initially only roughly hewn, and later beveled and slightly sharpened at the edge. Its profile changed from being curved on both sides to being rhombus-shaped and then triangular (Fig. 54, 55). Its cutting edge remained oval, reminiscent of the long oval cutting edges of the obliquely cut bone and antler implements (Figs. 25-27, 39e, g). Such degenerated specimens with a rectangular, "megalithic" cutting edge, like the one shown in Fig. 56, belong to the Later Neolithic period. In central Sweden, this civilization stretched from Bohuslän eastwards to the Baltic coast and somewhat beyond the northern border of central Sweden up to Gästrikland, and also

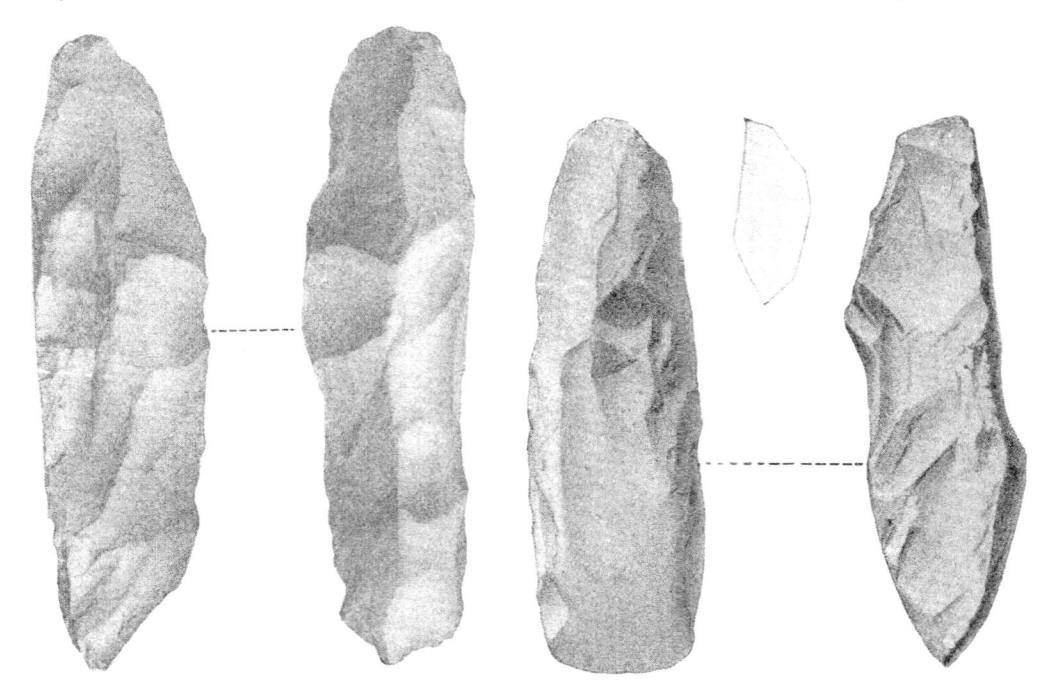

Fig. 55: ¹/₂. Genuine Nøstvet-Lihult axe. a) Side view, b) Top view. Cutting edge showing traces of grinding at the bottom. Jarlsberg and Laurvik. The illustration unfortunately depicts an inverted orientation.

Fig: 56: ¹/₂. Degenerated Nøstvet-Lihult axe of the Late Neolithic period with rectangular cutting edge and trapezoidal cross-section.

southwards to Scania where it extended northward along the east coast to the eastern county of Kalmar. In Norway, its center was the Kristianiafjord, and it continued along the west coast from Kristiansund all the way to the Arctic Circle[1].

During the time that corresponds to the time of the earlier shell middens of the Ellerbek people, the Lihult axe of the Dobbertiners evolved in the Kristianiafjord, in central Sweden, and in the county of Kalmar from its

---

[1] For this and the following see also *Mannus* I, 1909: "Urfinnen und Urincogermanen," I.

characteristic triangular shape into an oval-shaped round-butted axe[1], which was also not made of flint but of solid rock, but during that same time its cross-section was still sharpened at least along the cutting edge, and initially, like all Early Neolithic (or Mesolithic) axes, it still had a tongue-shaped cutting edge, but later on it only had a slightly curved, narrow (Fig. 57) cutting edge. The latest of its forms, with a broadly oval profile and a rectangular, very broad cutting edge (Fig. 58), which then culminated in the rock axe's transition from the round-butted axe to the point-butted rock axe (Fig. 59), is dated to an even later period of the Scandinavian Dobbertin population. They still fished on lakes then, but this

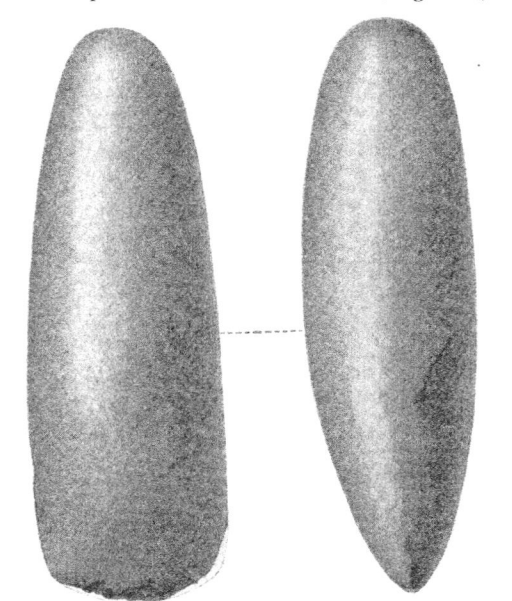

Fig. 57: ¹/₂. Narrow-edged round-butted axe.   Fig. 58: ¹/₂. Broad-edged round-butted axe.

had now shifted from the water level to the shore. Their distribution extended over the whole of eastern Sweden from Scania to Uppland and further afield to Åland. Their civilization is called the "Dwelling-Place civilization" or earlier "Arctic" civilization, which was contemporaneous with the second stage of the Indo-Germanic large stone tombs, the so-called earlier passage graves (about 3500–3000 BC). The round-butted axes spread by way of Denmark into northeastern Germany to the remnants of the local Dobbertiners who were free of Indo-Germanic domination, and particularly in Brandenburg we find these axes in their earlier, oval-edged forms, whereas the later forms are found in

---

[1] N. Åberg: "Kalmar läns Stenålder." Kalmar 1913 (*Meddelanden från Kalmar läns fornminnes förening* VII), pp. 13–30.

Pomerania and particularly frequently in East Prussia (and here in association with peculiar pottery, which appears to have been a hybrid of the Northern Indo-Germanic and Pre-Finnic styles).

Just as the Ellerbekers spoke a Pre-Indo-Germanic language, the language of the people of the Dwelling-Place civilization was a Pre-Finnic one.

The eastern Swedish Dwelling-Place civilization of this time already had coarse ceramic vessels with a characteristic pit ornamentation, as well as with the so-called comb ornamentation and the pattern of vertical zigzag rows or horizontal rows of diagonal impressions, a borrowing from the ceramics of the Indo-Germanic Megalithic culture of southern Sweden, albeit only in its crudest forms (Fig. 60). However, they still did not know of agriculture, and only on Gotland had their breeding of domesticated animals advanced beyond the Dobbertiner Arctic Spitz or true wolfhound[1], which was an inheritance from the Ancylus period. Here, as a result of the influence of the neighboring Indo-Germanic Megalithic civilization, the small bog swine

Fig. 59: ¹/₂. Transition from the broad-edged round-butted axe to the point-butted axe made of solid rock.

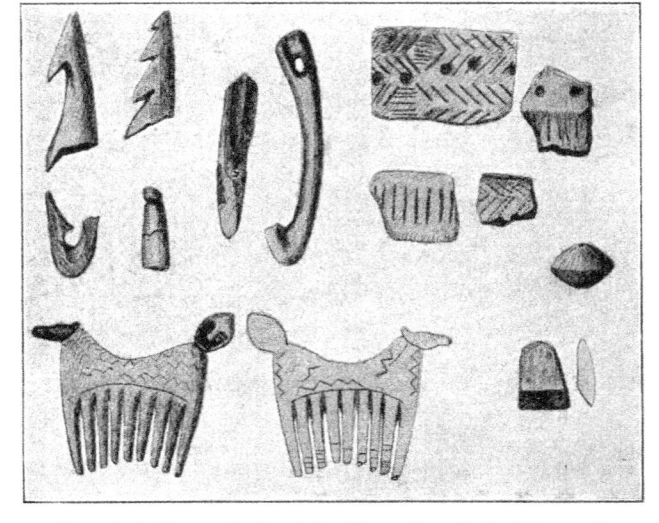

Fig. 60: Gullrum, Gotland dwelling-place finds (*Mannus* I).

---

[1] As the premier expert on our mammals, Prof. Matschie has informed me that the Arctic wolfhound was of the same type as the so-called police dogs, which have today suddenly become such an astonishingly popular breed.

(*Torfschwein*)[1] is found in abundance at the sites of Hemmor, Gullrum, and Visby. On the other hand, through its abundant figurative representations and sculptures, which were true to life in the depiction of animals (Figs. 61-63), but

Fig. 61: ¹/₁. Moose made of clay.

Fig. 62: ¹/₁. Moose head made of clay.

(Åloppe, Uppland, Sweden.)

much less so in the depiction of people (Figs. 63-65)[2], the Dwelling-Place civilization demonstrated its connection with the civilization of the Ancylus period (Figs. 15, 27), even for those researchers who believe that the realistic depiction of animals was only a consequence of the cultural character of hunters and fishers. In particular, the two large game animals, the moose and the bear, as well as the hunting companion, the dog (Fig. 63), were preferred in these depictions for ritualistic purposes of conjuring magic effects during the hunt. Ailio places the Arctic sculpture of central Sweden on the one hand, and that of Finland and Russia on

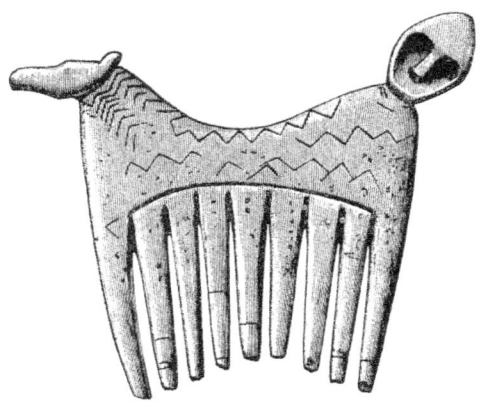

Fig. 63: ²/₃. Gullrum, Gotland. Bone comb.

---

[1] Pira: "Studien zur Geschichte der Schweinerassen, insbesondere derjenigen Schwedens" (*Zoologischen Jahrbüchern*, Suppl. 10, Heft 2. Jena 1909.)

[2] It is most remarkable that at the site of a somewhat later settlement at Jettböle on Åland, in addition to clay figures of animals, 60 clay idols were found, some representing males and some representing females, with some similar in shape to the East Prussian flat amber figures, while others were more similar to clay idols specific to the Southern Indo-Germanic civilization of the lower Danube; see Björn Cederhvarf: *Finska Fornminnesföreningens Tidskrift* 1912, 26, pp. 307 ff. with 8 plates. — Recently, such clay human idols have also been discovered at the Stone Age settlements near Kaukola and Räisälä on the Karelian isthmus between Lake Ladoga and the Gulf of Finland; see Sakari Pälsi: "Riukjärven ja Piiskunsalmen kivikautiset asuinpaikat Kautolossa" (*Finska Fornminnesföreningens Tidskrift* 1920, 28, pp. 166 ff., Plate XIX).

the other, as having been under the influence of connections with East Prussia, whose amber in the form of figurative representations (Figs. 66–72) was in the Nordic-Arctic region introduced to both Sweden and Finland (Fig. 65), and was also independently replicated in both of these areas thereafter[1].

The same connection with the civilization of the Ancylus period is demonstrated by a series of hunting implements: points with and without barbs on the sides, harpoons with barbs on one side or both sides, chisels, knives, awls, and also fish hooks, which by then already had the barb on the front of the tip, and which were all made of moose bone or moose antlers (Fig. 60, top left). There were also weapons made of solid rock: the round-butted axe in its very latest form, as well as the so-called Vespestad axe, which is polished on all sides with a sharpened edge on one side, that is, a transverse axe, and the small Gullrum chisel or its later variant, the Vittinge chisel (Vespestad in Jæderen in western Norway, Gullrum on Gotland, Vittinge in Uppland: Fig. 60, bottom right).

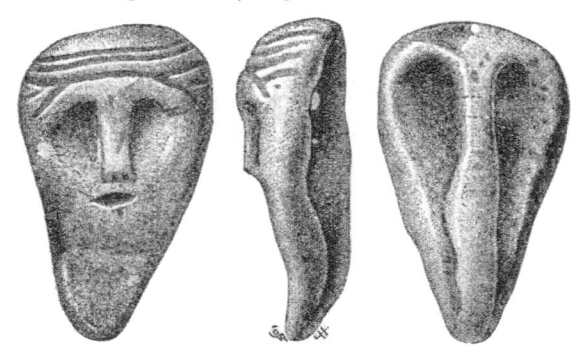

Fig. 64: ¹/₁. Västergötland. Amber amulet.

Fig. 65: ¹/₁. Sakkola near Viborg, Finland. Amber pendant.

It is necessary here to provide a brief overview of the times and locations in which the gradually increasing encroachment of the Indo-Germanic agricultural Megalithic population into the territory of the Pre-Finnic fisher and hunter population of the Dwelling-Place civilization took place.

A more precise knowledge of these changing conditions than existed in 1908 (the year when I wrote my lecture on Proto-Finns and Proto-Indo-Germanics) only came about through the most precise statistics-gathering and mapping that has been carried out in Sweden over the past decade for the Stone Age finds from

---

[1] J. Ailio: "Zwei Tierskulpturen" (*Finska Fornminnesföreningens Tidskrift* 26, 1912, pp. 257 ff.); see also A. W. Brögger: *Den arktiske Stenalder i Norge*. Kristiania 1909, pp. 185 ff., 226 ff.

several particular landscapes[1]. Geology has rendered an invaluable service to archaeology here. As is well known, only after the Ice Age did Scandinavia begin to gradually emerge from the sea until finally reaching its present form and relative elevation at the end of the Stone Age. Thus the different elevation layers

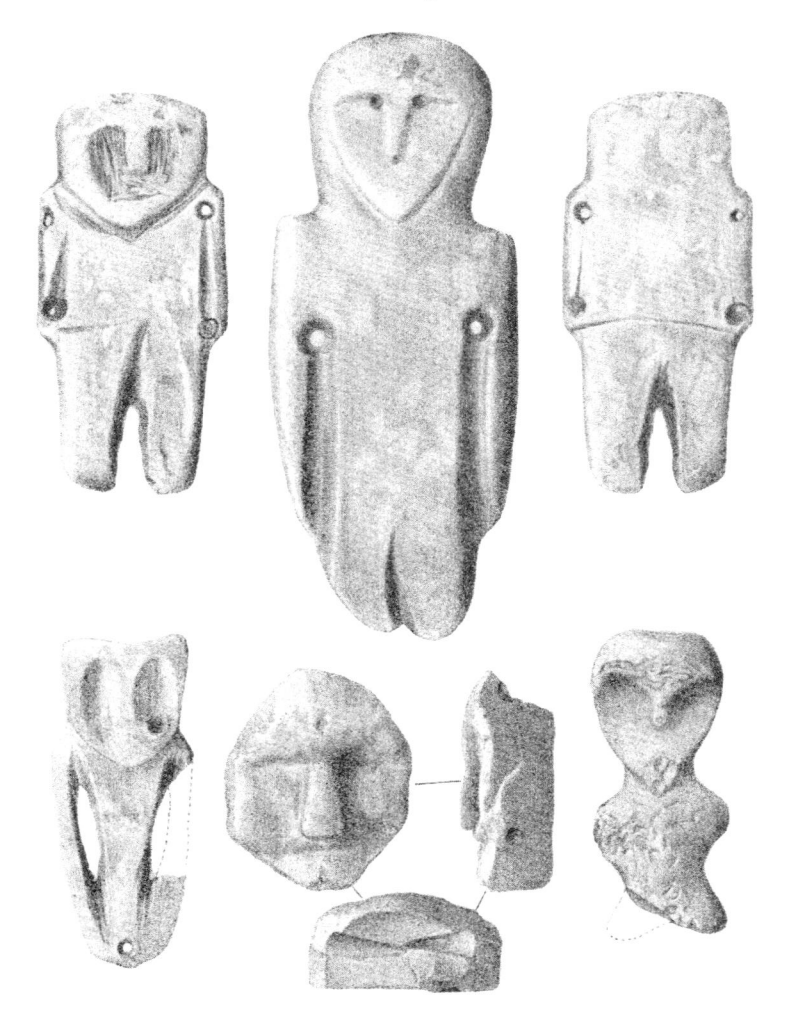

Figs. 66–71: ¹/₂. Schwarzort, Curonian Lagoon, East Prussia. Amber idols.

of these lands provide an excellent chronometer for determining what was its earliest settlement. Elevation maps are now used, on which the gradual elevation of the land above the level of the earliest prehistoric periods is indicated by isobase lines, in order to record the locations of the tools from the different

---

[1] See Oscar Almgren: "De pågaende Undersökningarna om Sveriges första Bebyggelse" (*Fornvännen* 1914, pp. 1 ff.).

Fig. 72: Bernburg: Amber idol.

periods of the Stone Age[1]. This has resulted in a complete agreement between the results of geology and those of archaeology, a truly spectacular confirmation of the correctness of the methods of both sciences, in particular for the relative determination of the dates of archaeological finds based on the evolution of their forms ("typology"): this is not a confirmation that we are experiencing here for the first time, however, but rather one that we have continuously been receiving for several decades. In the same order that archeology has determined for the evolutionary development of the stone axe, its different forms succeed each other on the landscape according to the different elevation levels on which they are found: each later form is spread over a larger area than the next earlier one, and always over that area which had been above the waterline during its corresponding period.

To go even deeper into detail[2], then for example in Närke it can be shown that the earlier round-butted axes lie approximately on the line 60m above the sea, the

---

[1] The first step in this direction was made in 1901 by Artur Hollender ("Om Sveriges Nivåförändringar efter Människans Invandring": *Geologiska Föreningens Förhandlingar* Bd. 23) with the evidence he provided of the differential distribution of axes without shaft holes and shaft hole battle axes.

[2] To date, the following presentations and statistical reports on the particular Swedish landscapes during the Stone Age have been published:

1. Birger Nerman: "Östergötlands Stenålder" (*Meddelanden från Östergötlands Fornminnes förening* 1911). Linköping 1911.

2. Sune Lindquist: "Från Nerikes Sten- och Bronsålder" (*Meddelanden från Föreningen Örebro Läns Museum.* V.) Orebro 1912.

3. Nils Åberg: "Kalmar Läns Stenålder" (*Meddelanden från Kalmar Läns Fornminnesförening* VII.) Kalmar 1913.

4. Sigurd Erixon: "Stenåldern i Blekinge" (*Fornvännen* 1913, pp. 125 ff.).

5. Ernst Nygren, "Värmlands Stenalder" (*Värmland förr och nu* XII. 1914, pp. 19 ff.) Karlstad 1914.

6. Nils Lithberg, *Gotlands Stenålder*. Stockholm 1914.

7. K. E. Sahlström: *Om Västergötlands Stenålders bebyggelse. Akademisk Avhandling*. Stockholm 1915.

K. E. Sahlström: "Förteckning över Skaraborgs Läns Stenåldersgravar." Mariestad 1915. (*Västergötlands Fornminnesförenings Tidskrift* III.)

8. Eskil Olsson: "Stenåldern i Västmanland, Dalarne och Gästrikland" (*Ymer*. Stockholm 1917, pp. 105 ff.)

Eskil Olsson: *Förteckning öfver tillvaratagna Sten- och Bronsålderfynd i Västmanland, Dalarne och Gästrikland*. Västerås 1917.

9. For Uppland, a depiction of its Stone Age has been published in: *Upplands Fornminnesföreningens Tidskrift*, Heft 26, Uppsala 1909. Additionally:

10. J. V. Erikson: "Studier över Upplands förhistoriska Geografi," *Upplands Fornminnesföreningens Tidskrift*, Heft 29, 1913.

11. A. G. Högbom: "Studier öfver Upplands äldre Bebyggelsehistoria" (*Ymer* 1912, pp. 255 ff.).

later round-butted axes a little lower, the thin-butted axes of the Dolmen period at 45–40m, the implements of the Passage Grave period 40–25m, the earlier Arctic dwelling-places (like Åloppe, Gullrum) 38–32m, and from the complete tail-end of the Stone Age the flint daggers and completely degenerated simple shaft-hole work axes are found only in the lowest landscapes, for example in the lake shores which only emerged due to the lowering of the water level of Lake Hjälmar, while from below Lake Hjälmar's river outlet there are no finds from the Stone Age at all.

And the pattern is the same in Uppland, Västmanland, and especially also in Bohuslän, which along its coast was uncommonly rich in settlements, which will be demonstrated by the long-term research in Bohuslän of the late Gabriel Wilhelm Ekman, the results of which remain unpublished as of yet[1]. On Gotland's coast the so-called Limhamn axe type, which is attributed to the time of the shell middens, lies exactly at the elevation of the temporally corresponding highest coastline during the Littorina stage of the Baltic Sea.

Where there was no advance of the coast as a result of land uplift, such as in Blekinge and Kalmar County, or where the first settlements were on a larger lake, such as in western Östergötland (Lake Vättern) or in Västergötland (Lake Vänern), settlement spread from the coasts and shores and gradually extended inland. In Västergötland the early Lihult axe (p. 35) has been found in the immense quantity of about 600, mainly in the northwest of the landscape on the lower Göta älv and on the southwestern tip of Lake Vänern, where it represents an expansion of the population of the even earlier-settled Bohuslän to the west, and in turn from there we trace these axe finds northeastward to Närke and Östergötland, where the earliest settlement is revealed. Later, the imported flint axe suddenly intruded into Västergötland from the southwest, and from then on along with its associated Megalithic tomb civilization it dominated the interior of the landscape, in the Silurian region of Falbygden and Valle. The long-settled northwestern parts, on the other hand, then saw their population withdraw from the coast and head further and further upstream and inland, and their stone tools suffered the strongest influence from the flint tools of the newly arrived Megalithic population, until the Stone Cist period when there then was dense settlement throughout the entire landscape, but in such a way that the form of the stone cist grave was predominant almost throughout, while on one side the solid

---

[1] Oscar Almgren in: *Oldtiden* VII. Kristiania 1916, p. 190.

rock shaft hole axes predominated, and on the other side, on the northern half of the landscape, only the flint daggers were predominant.

This aforementioned shift of settlement conditions, which in Västergötland, as in all landscapes south of the Dal River, changed from a seacoast and lakeshore settlement to one of the fertile inner plains, represents the displacement of the Pre-Finnic fisher and hunter population by the Indo-Germanics who practiced agriculture and animal husbandry. Only at the southernmost tip of Sweden in Scania were the (Arctic) dwelling-places of the fisher population not on the seacoast, but only on lakes, since the Ellerbeker Pre-Indo-Germanics dominated the coast there. On the other hand, further north, both what then constituted the west coast of Halland and Bohuslän as well as what was then the east coast of Blekinge, Östergötland, Södermanland, and Uppland were filled with the Pre-Finnic fisher population, as were the coasts of Gotland. As was noted earlier, this was the case during the earlier and middle Passage Grave periods. Then, with the exception of a few even later highland dwelling-places (Torp and Ingarö) and the island of Stora Karlsö near Gotland, there is a sudden disruption of the "Arctic" Dwelling-Place civilization, although nowhere here does the full Megalithic culture then move in. For the passage graves are everywhere missing here, with the exception of Öland. Only the stone cists, which mark the end of the Stone Age, were evenly distributed across all of the landscapes.

In the north of Scania on the east coast and further on into Blekinge, the flint intrusion seems to have more of the character of something imported through trade, rather than one of something brought in by a newly invading population.

In Kalmar County, the earlier-populated east coast, which with the thousands of discoveries of round-butted axes along the short stretch north from Kalmar to Oskarshamn was home to the fisher population, was sharply delimited from the area to the south of Kalmar extending to the border of Blekinge and which still encompassed central Öland, which is just as rich in discoveries of both thin-butted and thick-butted flint axes. What is striking is the complete lack of "Arctic" dwelling-places in Kalmar County. The flint civilization and that of the battle axes made of solid rock from the later Passage Grave period, which often stand in stark ethnic contrast to one another, were widespread everywhere in Kalmar County without any such contradiction, and in the Stone Cist period a balance between the two civilizations was almost completely achieved, aside from a vastly greater prevalence of the flint daggers in the early flint area compared to the early Pre-Finnic area. The flint exported from Scania must have therefore bypassed Blekinge on its way to Öland and Kalmar, that is, it must have arrived by sea, and thereby led to the displacement of fisher culture in those areas much earlier than in Blekinge.

On Gotland, the flint civilization had been cleaving apart the ancient coastal population since the Dolmen period, having been carried by an invading population, for the areas of the two civilizations are markedly dissimilar. In the Passage Grave period, however, the Arctic coastal dwelling-places laid in the same area as those of the flint civilization. Nevertheless, it would be absurd to cite Lithberg and declare these sites to have been the fishing places of the agricultural population of the flint civilization, since the civilizations were so very different. For here, as with everywhere else, the flint civilization demonstrated a complete mastery of agriculture and livestock breeding, but the fisher population had a grasp of neither, with the exception of the aforementioned breeding of bog swine (pp. 38 f.).

As for Östergötland, we have already mentioned the fisher population which dwelled on the coast, especially on the northern shore of Bråviken Bay, as well as the already very early and extensive intrusion of the flint culture into the westward fertile Silurian region. But here the round-butted axe is also discovered very abundantly in some places, such that the picture of the settlement conditions in this area is not so distinct and clear. Even the renowned pile-dwelling at Alvastra contains a mixture of "Arctic" Dwelling-Place ceramics and southern Scandinavian Indo-Germanic ceramics.

In the landscapes of ancient Svealand, Södermanland, and Uppland, the situation was the same as in Blekinge, that is, there was only a gradual infiltration of the Indo-Germanic civilization of Southern Scandinavia, in that the flint was probably introduced only through trade, and the solid rock implements underwent their transformational development and evolution while under the influence of the Indo- Germanic forms of flint implements.

We now wish to verify by means of an anthropological investigation that which has just been demonstrated by archaeological means.

As has been shown in the preceding pages, the Dobbertin population of the Ancylus period was evenly divided between the long-skulled and short-skulled branches of the Western European racial strain, while the long-skulled branch seems to have been strongly predominant among the bearers of the Ellerbek civilization of the Littorina period. As the Ellerbek people advanced into the previously completely unsettled areas to the west, south, and north, the

Dobbertiners were gradually surrounded by the Ellerbek people, at first by being circumvented, and later also by being driven out of their settlements. The bolder, more resolute segments among the Dobbertiners, that is, the more long-skulled ones, must have escaped these clutches by emigrating, while the more indolent and weaker-willed segments, that is, the more short-skulled ones, must have submitted to Ellerbeker domination, and later, in some places much later, gradually began to mix with them.

Such a mixture did not occur within Västergötland until almost the end of the Stone Age because, as we have established, the descendants of the Ellerbekers, the Megalithic population, settled in a completely different area than the earlier-settled descendants of the Dobbertiners. We observed the same phenomenon for Kalmar County as well as Öland. It is therefore easy to recognize that the very numerous skeletons (50) from the stone graves of Västergötland (plus Bohuslän) and Öland belong almost exclusively to the purely long-skulled Nordic racial type[1]. Only three skulls provide exceptions: one from the Slutarp dolmen (No. 23 in Fürst), which with a cephalic index 80.2 lies just on the cusp of the long-skulls and the short-skulls and is of the Borreby type (p. 49); a second, female, from one of the passage graves of Karleby[2] has the cephalic index 85.5 and is a quintessential Grenelle type; and a third from a stone cist in Hällekis[3] which has a cephalic index of 84.2 and is also of the Grenelle type. Two skulls from the stone cists in Närke are also indicative of the Nordic racial branch[4], although one, a female, has a cephalic index of 80.

Additionally, a few long-skulls are said to have been found in Östergötland, although nothing further about them has been published yet.[5]

The anthropological conditions were different in Scania and Gotland, with the latter being the only place in Sweden where we have found well-preserved remains of the Pre-Finnic population. In Scania, from Vellinge near Malmö, we have from single earth graves from the Stone Cist period, as well as from an actual stone cist, some skeletons that were described by Fürst. These deviate from the

---

[1] Gustaf Retzius: *Crania suecica antiqua*. German Edition. Stockholm 1900. — Carl M. Fürst: "Zur Kraniologie der schwedischen Steinzeit" (*Kungl. Svenska Vetenskapsakademiens Handlingar* Bd. 49: No. 1.) Uppsala and Stockholm, 1912.

[2] This is the passage grave excavated by Montelius and Retzius in 1872. The skull is listed by Retzius as No. 21, Plate 27.

[3] Retzius, *op. cit.*, No. 32.

[4] C. M. Fürst: *Fornvännen* 1914, pp. 17 ff.

[5] S. Lindquist: *Rig* 1918, p. 80.

purely Nordic type that was also predominant in Scania and in some cases also have higher cephalic indices: a female skull (II in Fürst) with a cephalic index 86.1 and with a "Finnish" structure, as the late Alfred Schliz had conferred to me at the time in writing (although it should be taken into account that Schliz understood the "Finnish" skull to be of the Tatar skull type), and two male skulls (I and III in Fürst) with cephalic indices of 79.3 and 81, of which the first represents a variant of the Borreby type, and the second a mixture between the Nordic and Borreby types.

Since only twelve Stone Age skulls have been documented in the small landscape of Scania, the percentage that these three short-skulls represent is many times larger than that of the three short-skulls from Västergötland. Moreover, the latter are also distributed across the entire period of megalithic tomb construction, that is, over at least one and a half millennia, while the three aforementioned Scanian graves belong exclusively to the end of the third millennium, that is, a time during which the Pre-Finnic Dwelling-Place population of the Scanian interior had been circumvented and surrounded by the Indo-Germanic Megalithic population of the Scanian coast and had already more or less anthropologically amalgamated with the Megalithic population. Archaeologically, the graves of Vellinge portray a civilization which was characterized by flint daggers, and which in its amalgamation of Indo-Germanic elements with Finno-Indo-Germanic (p. 78) elements already represented the beginnings of the Germanics.

Likewise, on Gotland the Dwelling-Place population did not substantially emigrate upon the invasion of the megalith people, but instead were resettled, as we have seen, within the very same boundaries that were imposed on them by the Megalithic population. Their skeletal remains here originate from the earlier Passage Grave period, to which the earlier Dwelling-Place civilization belongs. Here too, as was the case in Scania, we find cranial forms that deviate starkly from the Nordic type, even if, while it's not the most relevant fact with regard to our present anthropological view, the cephalic index of only one of the seven examined skulls from the site in Visby reaches the proportions of the Grenelle type, namely that of 85.1 for a female skull (XI in Fürst). However, this skull does not conform to the Grenelle type, but rather to the Borreby type (as per a letter I received from A. Schliz).

We will therefore be all the less surprised to learn that the only grave found outside of Sweden that belonged to the actively emigrating group of the Pre-

Finnic Dwelling-Place people, a crouched burial excavated in 1911 by Cederhvarf on the settlement of Jettböle on Åland, contained a long-skull that had a cephalic index of 73.8[1]. And finally, among the later Pre-Finns who migrated further east into the Olonets Governorate[2] and elsewhere in Russia, we also find representatives of the Nordic long-skulled race alongside other more divergent types[3].

These two cultures that had developed so differently, which we attribute to the Indo-Germanics on the one hand and to the Pre-Finns on the other, are primarily a reflection of the sharp contrast between two ethnic groups, which was a racial difference only insofar as the mixture of the two components of the Western European racial group in each of the two peoples differed, and which had probably also been subjected to disparate adaptations over the course of time.

This view of ours, which we have derived from the Swedish circumstances, is validated when we look further south to Denmark. Here too, as in southern Sweden, it was virtually impossible for the Pre-Finns to escape and emigrate once they were thoroughly surrounded by the Indo-Germanic settlements.

From the Danish islands, 166 Stone Age skeletons, including 158 skulls, have been examined by H. A. Nielsen[4]. Regrettably, he didn't examine any at all from Jutland. Nielsen distinguishes between five groups of skulls: two long-skulled and three short-skulled. He calls the long-skulled ones partly Cro-Magnon type and partly Avigny type. The Cro-Magnon type, generally known for its short, broad face, is in fact an orthocephalic, narrow-faced long-skull in Denmark; Nielsen's designation is therefore a misnomer. The so-called Avigny type differs from the former type by its generally narrower shape, steeper but not higher forehead, and a broad rounding of the less developed occipital protuberance, which in Nielsen's Cro-Magnon type protrudes in much more pointed fashion. The differences between the two types are therefore the same as what Alfred Schliz has more aptly

---

[1] Hj. Grönroos: "Stenåldersskelettfynden vid Jettböle på Åland" (*Finska Läkaresällskapets handlingar* LV, Nr. 4. Helsingfors 1913).

[2] For example at Lake Ladoga, see Alexander Alexandrovich Inostrantsev: *Der Mensch der Steinzeit an den Ufern des Ladogajees*. St. Petersburg 1882 (Russian).

[3] Carl M. Fürst: "Neolithische Schädel von der Insel Oesel" (*Baltische Studien zur Archäologie und Geschichte*. Berlin 1914, pp. 33 ff.): female short-skull from Kölljall (84.5) and a long-skull from Woisek (67.0) per R. Weinberg. See also: Kossinna: *Mannus* I, p. 48; R. Hausmann: *Sitzungsberichte der Gelehrten Estnischen Gesellschaft*. 1903, pp. 71 ff.; 1917, pp. 64 ff.

[4] H. A. Nielsen: "Yderligere Bidrag til Danmarks Stenaldersfolks Anthropologi" (*Aarbøger f. nord. Oldk.* 1911, Copenhagen, pp. 82 ff.)

called the wedge shape and the shield shape, whereby he was better able to distinguish the strongly sculptured facial profile from the weakly sculptured one, such as in the lateral view of the skull[1].

Among the short-skulled groups, which are always simultaneously narrow-faced and high-skulled, Nielsen distinguishes a group called Orrouy-Furfooz, which in the overhead view of the skull exhibits a short ovoid with its widest projection in the middle, very weak brow ridges, and a steep forehead, which extends into a single arch running back to the steeply sloped, rounded occiput. The second group of short-skulls is called the Møn type, a name derived from the island of the same name; but it is none other than the true Grenelle type, which differs from the Orrouy type in that in the overhead view it exhibits a short ovoid with its widest projection at the occiput, and the skull cap has a spherical shape, as well as particularly strong brow ridges with an indentation at the base. Finally, the last group is the well-known Borreby type, a blocky skull shape combined with a rather massive lower jaw, which otherwise resembles the Møn type, but which in the overhead view exhibits a pointed ovoid at the back of the skull and which is characterized by a recessed forehead.

Nielsen classifies 62 skulls as Cro-Magnon type (wedge shape), 19 as Avigny type (shield shape), 18 as Orrouy type, 14 as Møn type (Grenelle type), and 6 as Borreby type. Thus in Denmark we have 81 long-skulls and 38 short-skulls, whereas in Sweden we have 64 long-skulls and 6 short-skulls. Fürst then calculates for Sweden as a whole 91.4% long-skulls and 8.6% short-skulls, for Sweden excluding Scania 93.4% long-skulls and 6.6% short-skulls, but for the Danish islands including Scania 73.8% long-skulls and 26.2% short-skulls, for Scania alone 82% long-skulls and 18% short-skulls, and for the Danish islands alone 73.4% long-skulls and 26.6% short-skulls. So for eastern Denmark we have confirmed what we had also concluded for southern Sweden on both archaeological and anthropological grounds. The Danish islands (along with Scania and Gotland) represent an area where there was extensive mixing of the two branches of the Western European racial strain.

The final confirmation of this is provided by the anthropological conditions of the present day, which paint roughly the same picture as those of the Stone Age.

---

[1] Schliz: "Die vorgeschichtlichen Schädeltypen der deutschen Länder in ihrer Beziehung zu den einzelnen Kulturkreisen der Urgeschichte" (*Archiv für Anthropologie* N. F. VII, 1909, pp. 239 ff., IX, 1910, pp. 202 ff.); "die Vorstufen der nordisch-europäischen Schädelbildung" (*Archiv für Anthropologie* N. F. XIII, 1914, pp. 169 ff.).

The Bronze Age has left us very few skeletons due to the early arrival of cremation: 20 are known from Sweden, of which only 2 are very moderate short-skulls, and from Denmark, and from there almost exclusively from the tree-trunk coffins of Jutland, we know of only a dozen, only one of which is a short-skull. From the first millennium of the Iron Age we have no skeletal finds to speak of.

The picture is different for the later Iron Age, that is, the later period of the *Völkerwanderung* and onwards into the Viking Age. There we find a richer material tradition, yet we also arrive at different results. In Sweden there were 95% long-skulls and only 5% short-skulls during this time, and in Denmark only 3% short-skulls. This 5% of Swedish short-skulls, however, consists of only 3 specimens from Gotland (as opposed to 40 long-skulls). This corresponds entirely with the situation in Germany, where from the Merovingian period the astonishingly tall proto-German with a long Nordic skull, which is generally regarded as the genuine, true Germanic man in his typical form, appears almost without exception in the vastly numerous and grandest cemeteries known to archaeology. But the circumstances before and after show that during the Merovingian period, as a result of the centuries-long state of war which characterized the Völkerwanderung, a very special breed of mighty gargantuan warriors was cultivated in all Germanic lands, which made up a disproportionately higher percentage of the total population than had ever been found elsewhere. Only skulls from the central Swedish landscape of Södermanland and that of Dalsland in western Götaland can today still compete with those of the Merovingian epoch, as they still have 95% long-skulls, while Scania and Gotland have a respective 18% and 19% short-skulls, just like in the Stone Age, and Uppland has 21%, even more than the more northerly Västerbotten with its 19%, and is surpassed only by Lapland with its 23.67% shortheads (naturally we refer only to Swedish Lapland here). The only, admittedly remarkable, difference between the modern and the Stone Age Swedish skulls concerns the dimensions of the face: the Stone Age skull is narrow and long-faced, whereas the modern skull has a short face; according to the measurements taken in Dalarna and Västmanland, 76% have short faces and only 24% have long faces. It can therefore be said of the modern Swedes that the true Cro-Magnon type, that is, a long-skull with a broad face, predominates[1]. The complete dominance

---

[1] Gustaf Retzius and Carl M. Fürst: *Anthropologia suecica: Beiträge zur Anthropologie der Schweden*. Stockholm 1902.

of the long-skulls in the Merovingian period is one of the most striking proofs of the correctness of the racial-psychological law discussed on p. 27, which concerns the relationship between the longheads and the shortheads within one and the same race. During the more peaceful period of the Late Middle Ages, the Merovingian type of Germanic was, if not completely extinguished, then exceptionally diminished within the anthropologically different population of Germany as a whole; moreover, it also suffered severe declines in Denmark and southern Sweden.

In the Bornholm of today, L. Ribbing[1] arrived at a mean cephalic index of 80.3 for men and 80.6 for women, that is, after the necessary deduction of two units for measurements of living persons, which Ribbing had probably overlooked: 78.3–78.6, which indicates only a slight long-headedness, and which certainly encompasses a significant percentage of short-headed persons.

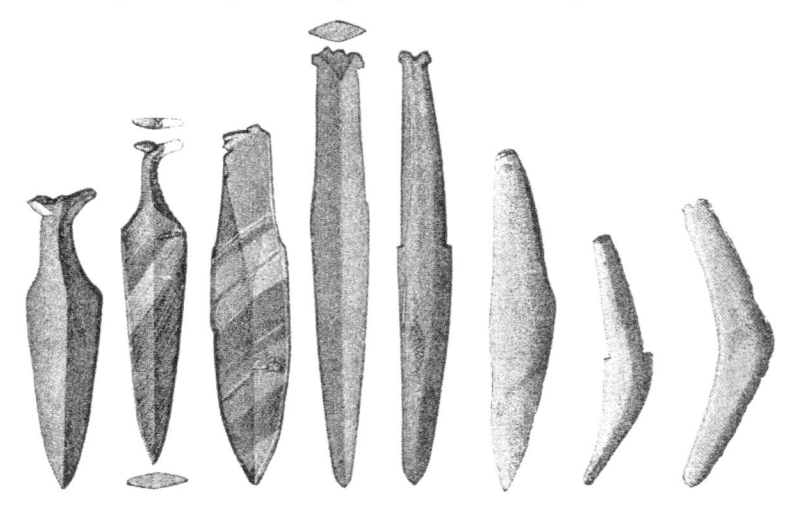

Figs. 73–80: ¹/₄. Swedish Norrland: Evolution of the double-edged Arctic slate knives (per Almgren).

When examining 400 people from northern Jutland and northern Funen, Sören Hansen[2] found that men had an average cephalic index of 80.6 and women had an average cephalic index of 81.4; however, the necessary deductions of two units required for comparisons with prehistoric skulls were probably not made here either, meaning that we arrive at an index that is only slightly higher than those found by Ribbing on Bornholm. Fürst has calculated the percentages for Denmark

---

[1] Ribbing: "Nogle Ord om Bornholms Antropologi" (*Meddelelser om Danmarks Antropologi* I, 2. Copenhagen 1908).

[2] Sören Hansen: "Om Hovedets Bredde-Indeks hos Danske" (*Meddelelser om Danmarks Antropologi* I, 2).

based on S. Hansen's figures: the proportion is 67% long-skulls and 33% short-skulls, although it should be noted that among the long-skulls only 12% are true long-skulls and 55% are medium-skulls.

For Norway, numerous unfortunately quite scattered works by Arbo and Larsen have demonstrated that the Borreby type is also found there along the entire coast, but inland, where the Nordic type generally predominates, only in the southwest, such as in Jæderen where it is the dominant type.

In western Jutland, northern Funen, and on the island of Anholt, H. P. Steensby[1] today distinguishes three skull types, the Nordic, the "Alpine" (which should be called the "Grenelle"), and the Borreby type. The blond, moderately short-headed Borreby type is even declared by him to be the most strongly represented.

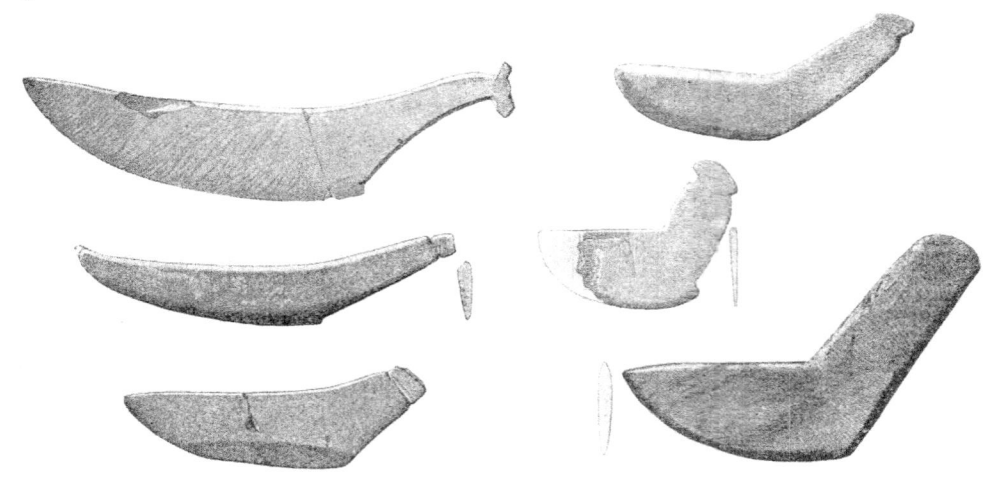

Figs. 81–86: ¹/₄. Swedish Norrland: Evolution of the single-edged Arctic slate knives (per Almgren).

With this we can conclude the anthropological examination of Scandinavia and Denmark, insofar as it is relevant to the interrelation between the Pre-Finns and the Proto-Indo-Germanics, and we can now turn our attention to the ensuing struggle between these two ethnic tribes.

Over the course of the middle Passage Grave period, the Pre-Finnic Dwelling-Place population, under pressure from the Indo-Germanic Megalithic population that was advancing from the south, burst forth across the Dal River to Swedish Norrland, where they established a flourishing slate industry. Noteworthy here

---

[1] H. P. Steensby: "Forelöbige Betragtninger over Danmarks Raceantropologi" (*Meddelelser om Danmarks Antropologi* I, 1. Copenhagen 1907).

are large slate knives, both double-edged (Figs. 73-80) and single-edged (Figs. 81 to 86), which initially featured naturalistic dog heads on their handles whose form would swiftly degenerate, as well as slate arrowheads with large barbs, which were apparently replicas of the flint arrowheads of the southern Swedish Megalithic civilization[1]. However, these earliest slate implements were also traded to the area south of the Dal River, and some of them were even recreated there[2], such that here, as in southern Norway, we may anticipate the presence of remains from the Pre-Finnic Dwelling-Place people that are yet to be discovered.

In the later Passage Grave period (3000-2400 BC), after being driven out of central Sweden in defeat, one segment of the Dwelling-Place people of Swedish

Fig. 87a, b, d: Earlier lance points and arrowheads; c, e: later double-edged knives.

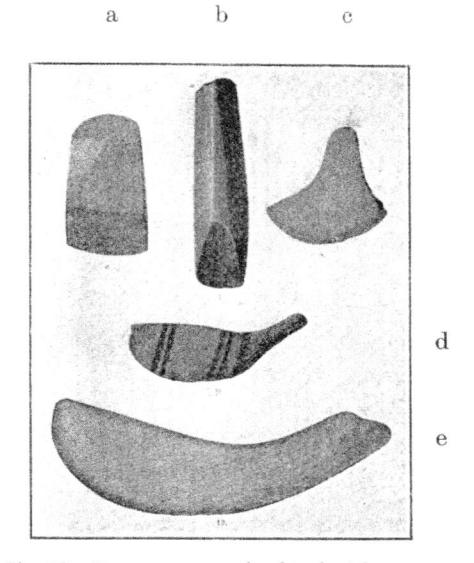

Fig. 88a: Transverse axe; b: chisel with concave edge; c, d, e: later single-edged knives.

Figs. 87, 88: $^1/_6$. Earlier and later Arctic civilization of Norway (per A. Rygh). Slate implements.

Norrland turned to the Trondheim Fjord and further northward along the Norwegian coast as far as Tromsø (Figs. 87, 88), while another segment headed to eastern Finland (Figs. 89-96). Characteristic of this later Arctic period is that both types of slate knives had by then lost any trace of the dog's head on the handle, which had been customary in earlier times, and had acquired a curvature that intensifies until they bend at right angles (Figs. 77-80, 83-86, 87e, 88c-e, 89), while the slate spearheads and arrowheads no longer retained their barbs (Figs. 90, 91).

---

[1] Sune Lindquist: *Från Nerikes Sten- och Bronsålder*. (Örebro 1912.), p. 50.
[2] Sune Lindquist: *Från Nerikes Sten- och Bronsålder*, p. 22.

Fig. 89: ¹/₂. Single-edged knife. (Kemijärvi near Uleåborg.)

Fig. 90: ¹/₄. Lance point or double-edged knife. (Karijoki near Vasa).

Fig. 91: ¹/₂. Arrowhead. (Lapua near Vasa).

Fig. 92: ¹/₂. Chisel. Kaukola near Viborg.

Fig. 93: ¹/₃. Chisel. (Pfielisjärvi near Kuopio.)

Fig. 94: ¹/₈. Rovaniemi pickaxe. (Rovaniemi near Uleåborg.)

Fig. 95: ¹/₈. Cradle-shaped pickaxe. (Tohmajärvi near Kuopio.)

Fig. 96: ¹/₄. Shaft-hole implement with extensions on the sides. (Pielisjärvi near Kuopio.)

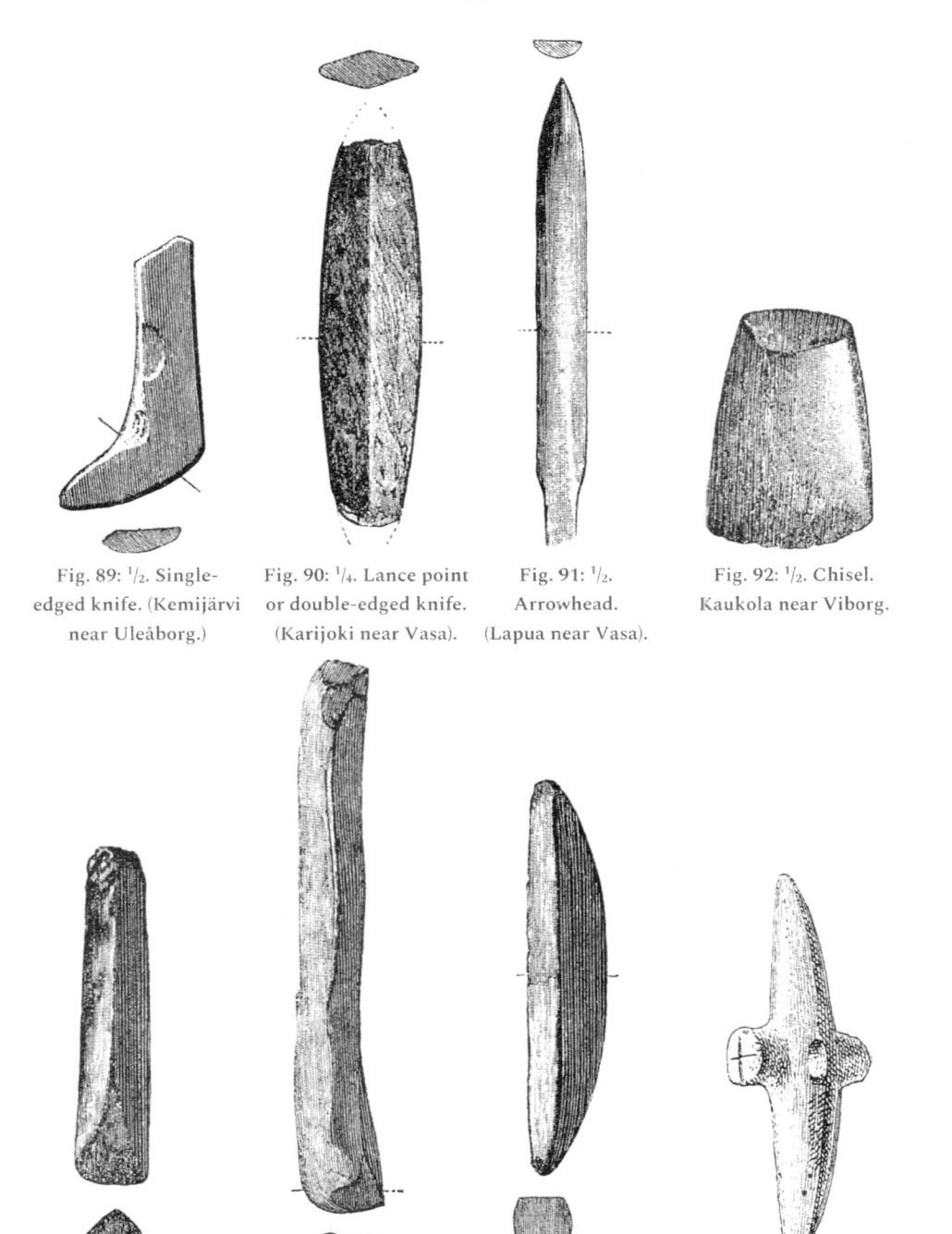

Figs. 89–96: Stone implements from Eastern Finland, most of which were made of slate (per Hackman).

Slate chisels, such as the earlier western Norwegian Vespestad type or the Upplandic Vittinge type (Figs. 92, 93) and massive slate pickaxes (Figs. 94, 95) also appeared everywhere, but there were no straight axes. Particularly noteworthy here as ornamental items were T-shaped slate pendants. The naturalistic animal rock carvings in Jämtland and on the Norwegian coast from Trondheim to Ofoten (Figs. 97–102)[1] also fall into this later Arctic period, and these were again exclusively dedicated to depicting the bear, the moose, and the reindeer.

According to Almgren, southwestern Finland, on the other hand, was conquered by the Finno-Indo-Germanic Boat Axe civilization of southeastern Sweden[2].

The Finnish researchers, of course, have recently derived the Boat Axe civilization of southwestern Finland from northeastern Germany, particularly from East Prussia, which is supported not only by the shape of the boat axes and other axes (as per Soikkeli)[3], but especially by this group's ceramic vessels, the globular vessels with cord decorations, Julius Ailio's so-called Alastaro pottery (Fig. 103)[4], which have only just recently been discovered. It does indeed seem to be significant that Jutlandic boat axes are completely absent east of the Oder, with the exception of the distinctive Eastern European forms called Fatyanovo battle axes (see Figs. 125₇, 127), which are also strongly represented in East Prussia, and which are characterized by their flat upper surface which is sharply offset against the curved side surfaces and the unevenly

Figs. 97, 98: Landverk, Jämtland, Sweden:
Moose and bear.
(Fig. 97: Photograph. Fig. 98: Illustration.)

---

[1] *Mannus* I, pp. 42 ff. — Recently, such sites have also been discovered in Kristiania, Drammen, and elsewhere in southern Norway (Just Bing: *Ord och Bild* 29. Stockholm 1920, p. 418). Norway had only received its first Indo-Germanic population from Kristiania at the very end of the Stone Age, and this population was already in the midst of a transformation into a type that was purely Germanic.

[2] Oscar Almgren: "Några svensk-finska stenåldersproblem" Stockholm 1912. (Special issue: *Antikvarisk Tidskrift för Sverige*, Del. 20, Nr. 1, pp. 8 ff.)

[3] Kaarle Soikkeli in: *Finska Fornminnesföreningens Tidskrift* 1912, 26, pp. 285 ff.

[4] Aarne Europaeus: *Finska Fornminnesföreningens Tidskrift* 1915, pp. 16 ff.; *Finskt Museum* 1915, pp. 10 ff.; 1916, pp. 45 ff.; 1917, pp. 471 f.

curved undersides, in which they resemble the latest of the Silesian battle axes. Their neck knob usually only extends downwards, as is seen on the Jutlandic boat axes, while on the Swedish boat axes (Fig. 104) it protrudes uniformly both upwards and downwards[1]. When I asked the foremost expert on European Stone Age battle axes, my friend Åberg, he told me that although he had not studied the Finnish boat axes first-hand, but was acquainted with them only through the literature, he thought there was no doubt that they should be grouped together with the Swedish ones, and not with the Fatyanovo ones. He also makes the same judgment

Fig. 100: Bøla: Drawing of a reindeer with characteristic antler shape.

Fig. 99: Bøla, Trondheim Fjord (Norway). Reindeer, to the right of the waterfall.

Fig. 101: Live reindeer with the same antler structure.

about the boat axes from Lithuania and the Baltic lands[2]. Nevertheless, I can't quite shake the feeling that the Finns have a clearer view here than do the Swedes.

When it comes to the Swedish Boat Axe civilization, it was itself a result of the mixture of Proto-Indo-Germanic and Pre-Finnic populations. From the Indo-Germanic Megalithic population it had acquired agriculture, animal husbandry, and the production of polished flint gouges, while from the Pre-Finnic population it acquired the single earth burial and the battle axe of inland Jutlandic origin (boat axe) made of solid rock (Fig. 104); furthermore, from the Oder region it had borrowed, albeit in a more refined form, fine ceramic vessels which were not

---

[1] Åberg: *Das nordische Kulturgebiet in Mitteleuropa während der jüngeren Steinzeit*, pp. 105 ff. — Åberg: *Die Typologie der nordischen Streitäxte*. Würzburg 1918 (Mannus-Bibliothek 17), pp. 42 ff. — Åberg: *Prähistorische Zeitschrift* IX, 1917, pp. 21 ff.

[2] *Prähistorische Zeitschrift* IX, 1917, p. 46.

Northern Indo-Germanic but Southern Indo-Germanic[1] (Figs. 105-107). This Boat Axe civilization spread from Scania into the counties of Blekinge and Kalmar as well as Öland, Östergötland, and Västmanland and then as far as Uppland and Gästrikland.

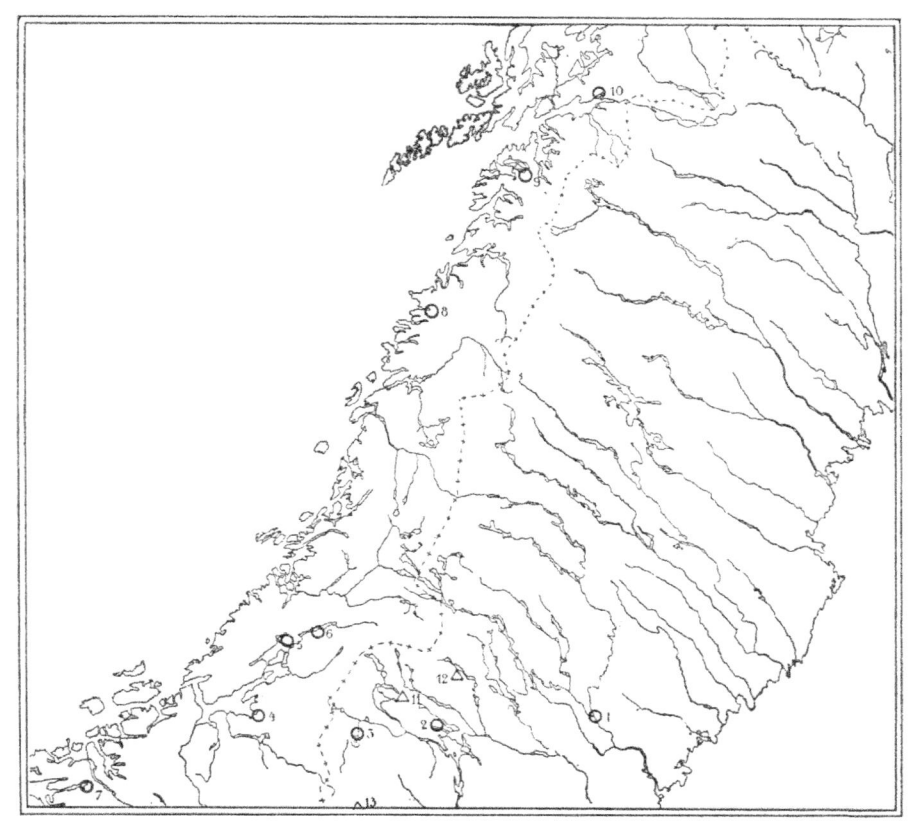

Fig. 102: Area of "Arctic" rock drawings (○ 1-10) and rock paintings (△ 11-13) in Scandinavia (per *Fornvännen* 1907).

At the closing of the Stone Age (Stone Cist period: 2400-2000 BC), proof of the fact that even at that time segments of the Pre-Finnic population had persisted in central Scandinavia is provided by the by no means slight backflows of weapons

---

[1] Oscar Almgren, *op. cit.*, pp. 27 ff. — Otto Frödin in: *Fornvännen* 1916, pp. 181 ff. — Gunnar Ekholm, on the other hand, instead sees the Swedish Boat Axe pottery as having originated from the northeastern German Corded Ware, from which he discovered an offshoot in a Boat Axe grave from Scania (Mus. Lund), which must be older than the typical southern Swedish Boat Axe pottery. Since Corded Ware pottery is also occasionally found in Upplandic settlements (Almgren, *op. cit.*, p. 34; Ekholm: *Upplands Fornminnesförenings Tidskrift*, H. 33, p. 19), Ekholm therefore concludes that the Alastaro pottery was indeed derived from northeastern Germany, but had made its way to southwestern Finland by way of Sweden (*Fornvännen* 1920, pp. 209 ff.).

and implements of eastern Finnish, northern Finnish, and Russian Karelian origin to central Sweden (Uppland) and southern Norrland (here we see this even during the Bronze Age), and to a much lesser extent to southwestern Finland which had by then been Finno-Indo-Germanicized by the Boat Axe civilization.

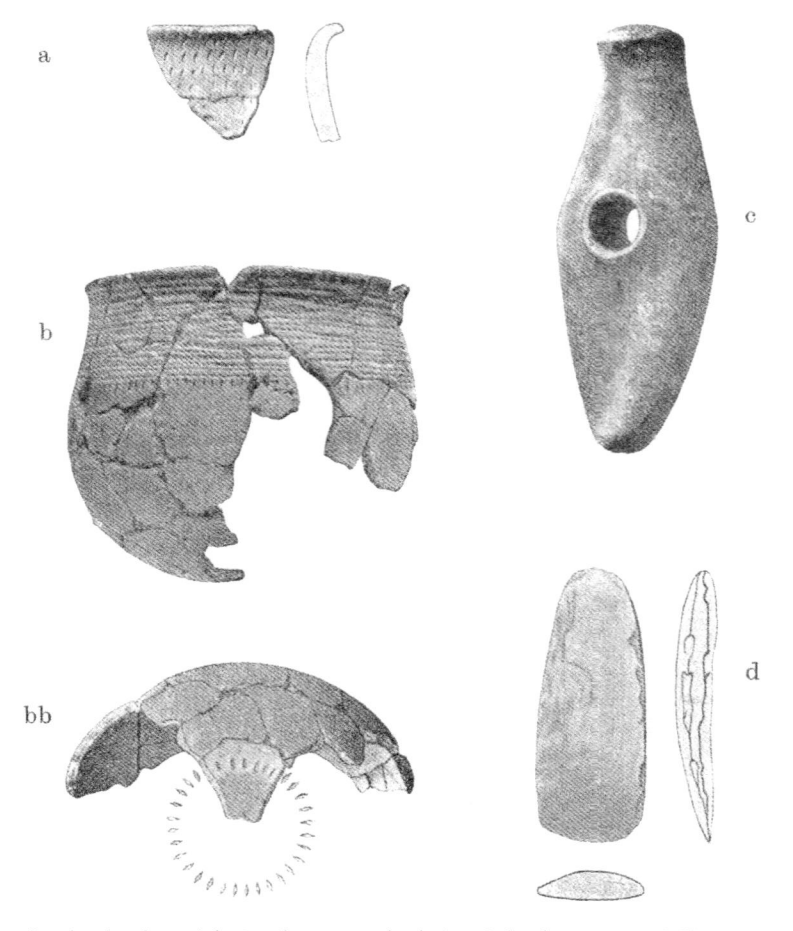

Fig. 103: Piirtola, Ilmola parish, Southern Ostrobothnia, Finland: Boat Axe civilization earth grave. a) $^1/_3$. pottery shards; b) $^1/_5$. clay vessel with cord decoration; bb) same, bottom view; c) $^1/_3$. boat axe; d) flint chisel.

Such imports from eastern Finland, or rather from Russian Karelia, included certain animal-head weapons with shaft holes, which were usually carved out of a massive potstone but were also in rare occasions crafted from hornblende slate. According to Ailio[1], around 20 such animal-head implements were known in 1920:

---

[1] J. Ailio: "Zwei Tierskulpturen" (*Finska Fornminnesföreningens Tidskrift* 1912, Bd. 26, pp. 259 ff.). — See also: O. Almgren: *Fornvännen* 1907, pp. 122 ff.; 1911, pp. 152 ff.

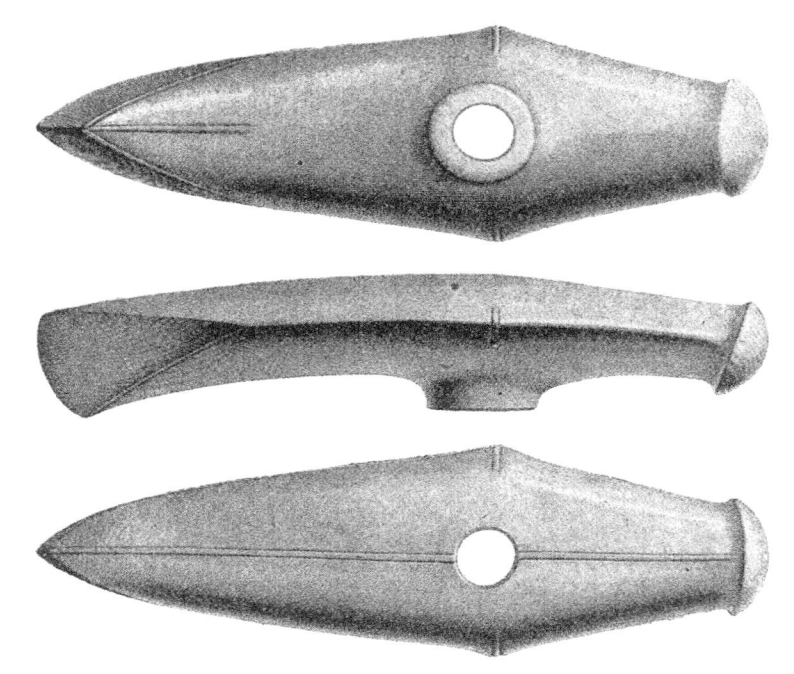

Fig. 104: ¹/₃. Södermannland (Sweden): Boat axe (per Montelius). Bottom view, side view, top view.

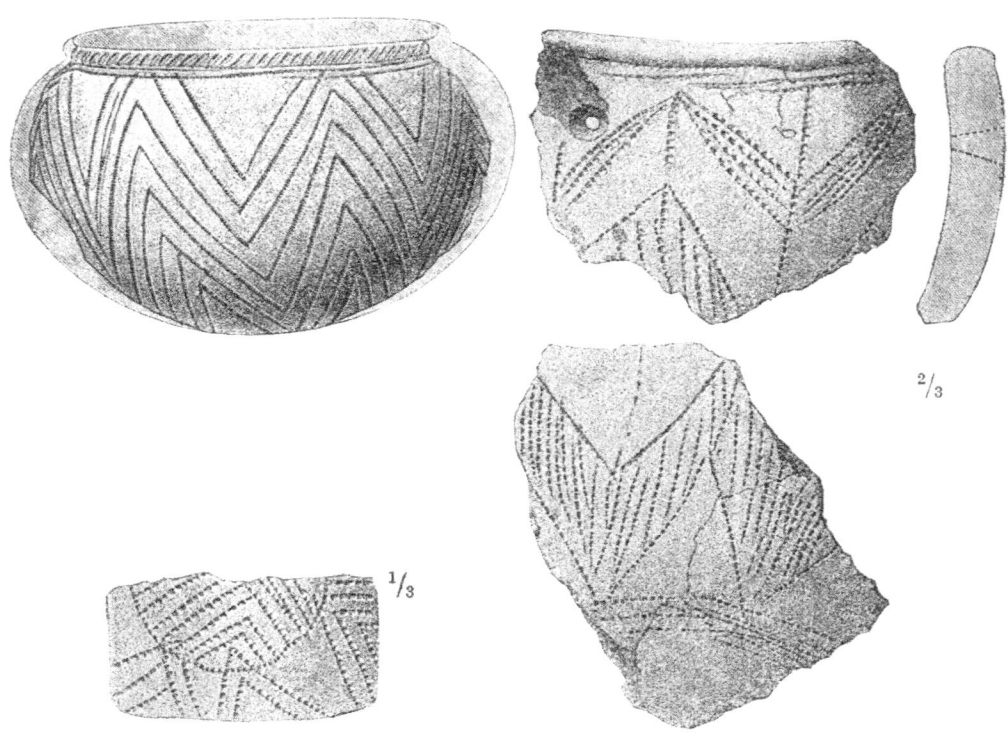

Fig. 105, 106: Swedish "band-pottery."
105. Östra Herrestad, Scania. 106. Olofsholm near Borås, Västergötland.

two from Sweden, seven from Finland, and eleven from Russia, with one of the latter being from the Arkhangelsk Governorate, and eight being from the Olonets Governorate, with almost all of these being found in the vicinity of Petrozavodsk. The large quantities of these Stone Age finds originating from the Olonets Governorate indicates that there was a fairly dense settlement there; half of all such stone implements are made of a type of tuff stone found near Petrozavodsk, and the potstone in question is also found in the same region; there are also Arctic rock carvings there that are of the same character as the previously discussed carvings from Jämtland and Norway (p. 55). Among all of such implements that

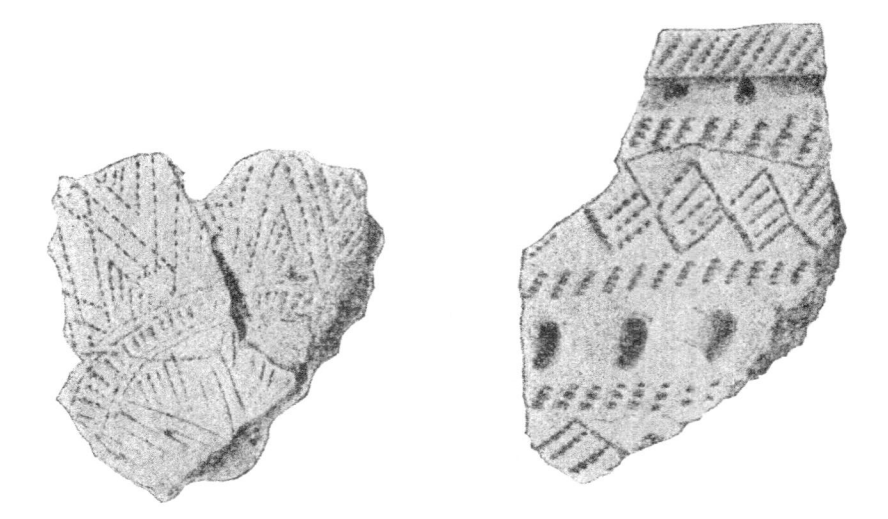

Fig. 107: ¹/₂. East Finnic comb ceramics. Räisälä, Finnish Karelia.

certainly originated in this region there are the rare examples consisting entirely of just an animal head, such as the magnificent moose head from Vittis in Finland (Fig. 108) and the bear head from Esbo in Finland (Fig. 116), but in most cases they feature both a head and a neck of some kind of animal, such as the pieces with a moose head from Säkkijärvi in Finland, Alunda in Swedish Uppland, and Padosero in Russian Karelia, (Figs. 109, 110, 113), or the one with a dog's head from Maaninka in Finland (Fig. 111), or those with a bear's head from Tulguba in Russian Karelia (Fig. 112) and from Antrea in Finnish Karelia (Figs. 114, 115). Given their overall nature and the contexts in which they were found, these items could not have actually been used as weapons, but instead only as implements used as votive offerings that would have been set up and displayed at hunting sites by means of wooden rods inserted into their shaft holes.

3. Pre-Finns and Proto-Finns in Eastern Europe

I shall now attempt to connect the beginnings and resettlements of the Proto-Finns, as deduced from the history of Finno-Ugric loanwords (as covered on p. 9), with the findings of Eastern European archaeology. Since what we are dealing with here involves explorations into uncharted territory, I must deviate somewhat from my usual terse style and provide a more elaborate presentation.

The distinctive "East Finnic" pottery of Stone Age eastern and northern Finland, that is, the main area of the Pre-Finns at the end of the Stone Age, which was perhaps derived from the pottery of the Pre-Finnic "dwelling-places" of eastern Sweden and which was certainly influenced by the later pottery of the Finno-Indo-Germanic Boat Axe civilization of southeastern Sweden (the so-called southern

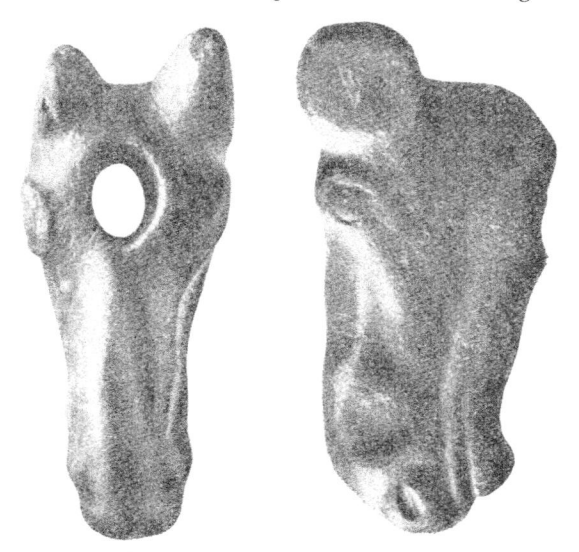

Fig. 108: ¹/₂. Vittis, Satakunta (Finland): Moose head weapon (per Ailio).

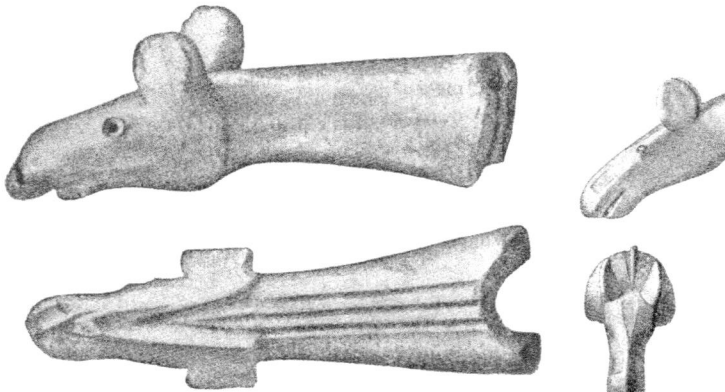

Fig. 109: ¹/₂. Säkkijärvi near Viborg, Finnish Karelia: Animal head weapon made of pot stone (per Tallgren).

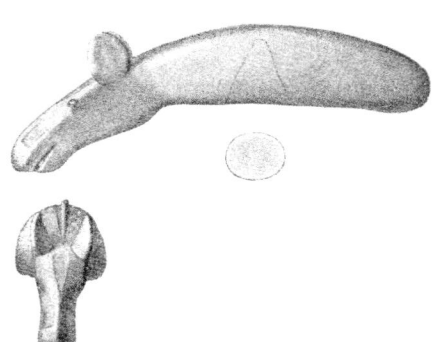

Fig. 110: ¹/₄. Alunda, Uppland (Sweden). Moose head implement made of pot stone (per Almgren).

Swedish "band-pottery"), is characterized by thick-walled vessels of coarse clay with rounded or more pointed bottoms, or much less frequently by those with flat bottoms, and especially by their decorative features (Figs. 117–119). This can be seen both from the deeply impressed pit ornamentation (an influence of the Dwelling-Place ceramics) and from the "comb ornamentation," which consists of densely packed, oblique parallel lines in a multilayered arrangement, which consist of individual shallow, mostly rectangular impressions (an influence of the southern Swedish "band-pottery" of the Boat Axe civilization): see Fig. 107 and the maps in Figs. 120, 121[1].

This type of ceramic vessel spread from eastern Finland and Karelia to Lake Ladoga, Lake Onega, and the White Sea, as well as to Estonia and Livonia and the governorates of Novgorod, Yaroslavl, Vladimir, Kostroma, Nizhny Novgorod, Kazan, Ryazan, Oryol, Poltava, and Kiev, and indeed even further afield to the Black Sea and the Caucasus and even across the Urals to western Siberia. It appears only at settlements whose archaeological remnants still appear to be strictly from the Stone Age[2]. Only at one settlement, namely that of Galich in the Kostroma governorate, is a more refined form of pottery found alongside this

---

[1] J. Ailio, who generally agrees with my views on the Finno-Ugric character of the Stone Age populations of northern Scandinavia, Finland, and northern and eastern Russia (*Monteliusfestschrift*. Stockholm 1913, p. 18), is unwilling to fully recognize Almgren's derivation of the "East Finnic" comb ceramics from the eastern Swedish pottery, but instead prefers to assume southern, i.e. northeastern German, influences here as well, to which he claims both eastern Sweden and eastern Finland were subjected. Nevertheless, I am not yet aware of any evidence that supports this view. I therefore endorse Almgren's interpretation for the time being. — There is also a second point on which I cannot agree with Ailio. The fact that the large, crude, cross-sectionally trapezoidal Rovaniemi pickaxes (Fig. 94), which have rounded upper and lower surfaces and are often sharpened at the cutting edge, as well as the sharply angled slate knives, occur frequently only in northern Finland, but are absent in eastern Finland (see map in Fig. 121), leads Ailio to identify northern Finland as having been a separate area of the Lapps that was distinct from those of the other Finno-Ugrians as early as the Stone Age. This is contradicted by the fact that the Lapps, as we have seen, are a Ugric tribe both in terms of race and the origin of their language, and that they do not appear to have joined the West Finns until the last millennium BC, at which point they thereby appear to have entered into the sphere of Scandinavian-Germanic influence (see pp. 7–10).

My view is further supported by the fact that the Lapps resemble the Samoyeds in almost all details of reindeer taming and breeding, even in those that are by no means dictated by nature, as U. T. Sirelius (*Journal de la Société Finno-Ougrienne* 1916, XXIII, 2) and G. Hatt (*Geografisk Tidskrift* 24, 1918) have demonstrated, contra K. B. Wiklund (*Ymer* 1918). All of these researchers consider the reindeer husbandry of the Lapps to date back to the Stone Age. However, it seems doubtful to me whether the presence of Stone Age Lapps in Tavastia can be deduced from the 2.21m long sled runner (Fig. 122a) which was discovered in the Saarijärvi district (northern Tavastia) and which was certainly from the Stone Age on account of the woodworking technique (small segment, Fig. 122b) and the deposits of vegetation found in the peg holes. It could have also belonged to other segments of the Finno-Ugrians. See also A. Europaeus: *Finskt Museum* 25. 1918, p. 30, Fig. 11 and J. T. Itkonen: "Teorier om renskötsels uppkomst" (*Finskt Museum* 26. 1919, pp. 30 ff.).

[2] J. Ailio: *Die steinzeitlichen Wohnplätze in Finnland*. Helsingfors 1909. I, pp. 81 ff. — A. M. Tallgren: *Die Kupfer- und Bronzezeit in Nord- und Ostrussland*. Helsingfors 1911. pp. 50 ff.

crude pottery, which had in turn spread over a large part of central Russia and which is called Fatyanovo pottery (Fatyanovo, Yaroslav governorate) after an

$1/4$	$1/6$	$1/8$	$1/5$	$1/4$
Fig. 111: Maaninka, Savonia, Finland. Dog's head weapon (per Ailio).	Fig. 112: Tulguba, Russian Karelia.	Fig. 113: Padosero, Russian Karelia. (per Aspelin.)	Fig. 114: Antrea, Russian Karelia.	Fig. 115: Antrea near Viborg, Russian Karelia. Bear head weapon.

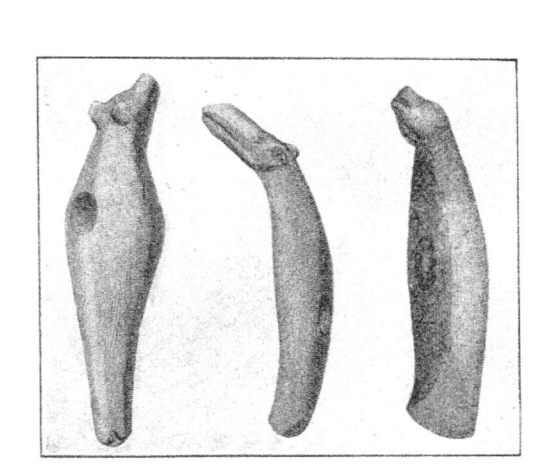

immensely significant burial ground where it and the rather advanced civilization associated with it were discovered. The presence of copper among this civilization need not prevent us from attributing it to the same period to which the settlements of eastern Finland with pit and comb ceramics belonged. We shall associate the vast dispersion of the latter with the dispersal of the Pre-Finns into eastern and southeastern Russia.

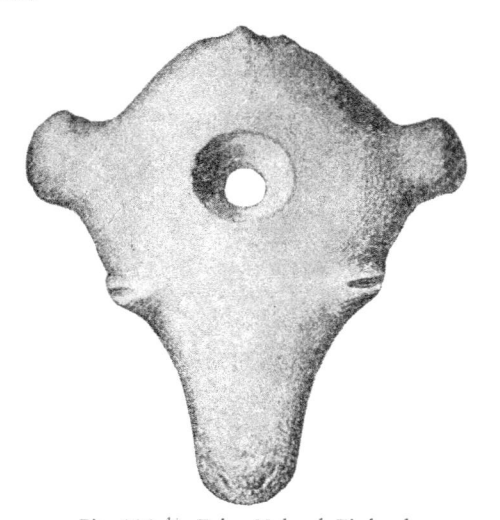

In contrast, the Fatyanovo civilization[1], which is represented in about 20 burial

Fig. 116: $1/3$. Esbo, Nyland, Finland: Degenerated bear's head (per Ailio).

---

[1] Tallgren: *ibid.* p. 45 and "L'âge du cuivre dans la Russie centrale" (*Finska Fornminnesföreningens Tidskrift* Bd. 32: 2, Helsingfors 1920).

grounds along the Oka and the area of the upper Volga to its north (Fig. 123), must be characterized by its "bomb-shaped" vessels (Fig. 125, No. 2, 3) which were derived from the globular flasks of eastern Germany (Fig. 124), by the eastern

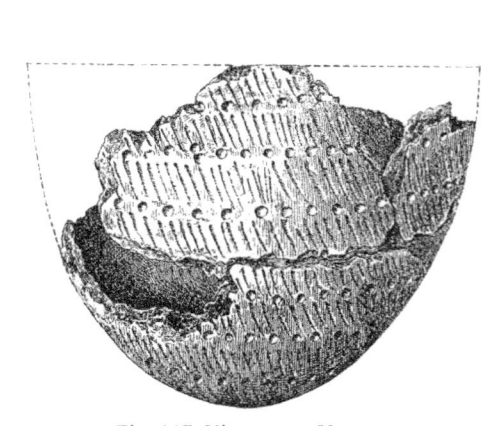

Fig. 117: Virrat near Vasa.

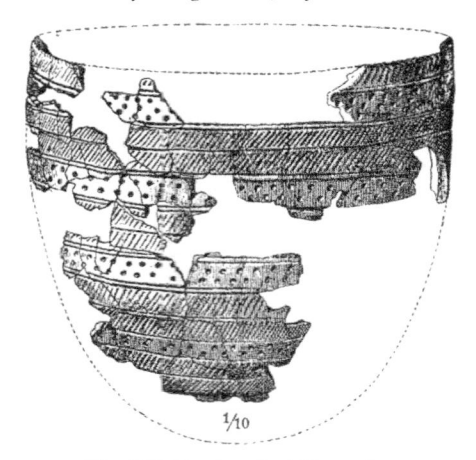

Fig. 118: Hankasalmi, Tavastia.

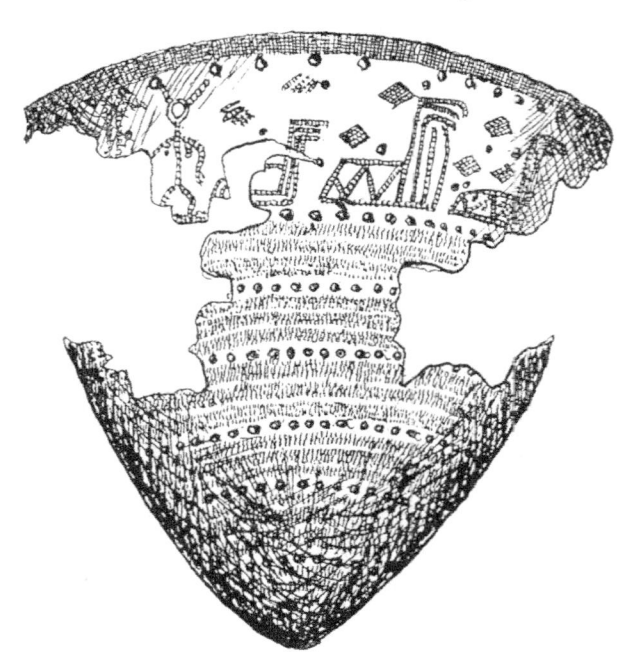

Fig. 119: Kolomtsy site on Lake Ilmen near Novgorod (per Peredolsky).

German forms of shaft hole battle axes made of solid rock (Figs. 125, No. 7; 127), namely in the form of the later boat axes (even one made of copper in one find shown in Fig. 126), by the thick-butted flint axes (Fig. 125, No. 6), by the amber and animal tooth jewelry (Fig. 128), and by the crouched burials in single earth graves which were protected by a stone ring (Fig. 125, No. 1), all of which can be attributed to the vast flow of population and culture from the second and third waves of Northern Indo-Germanic migration from the Vistula region to western and southern Russia, which I have conclusively substantiated, and which had also swept over central Russia's Pre-Finnic population. The basal Pre-Finnic

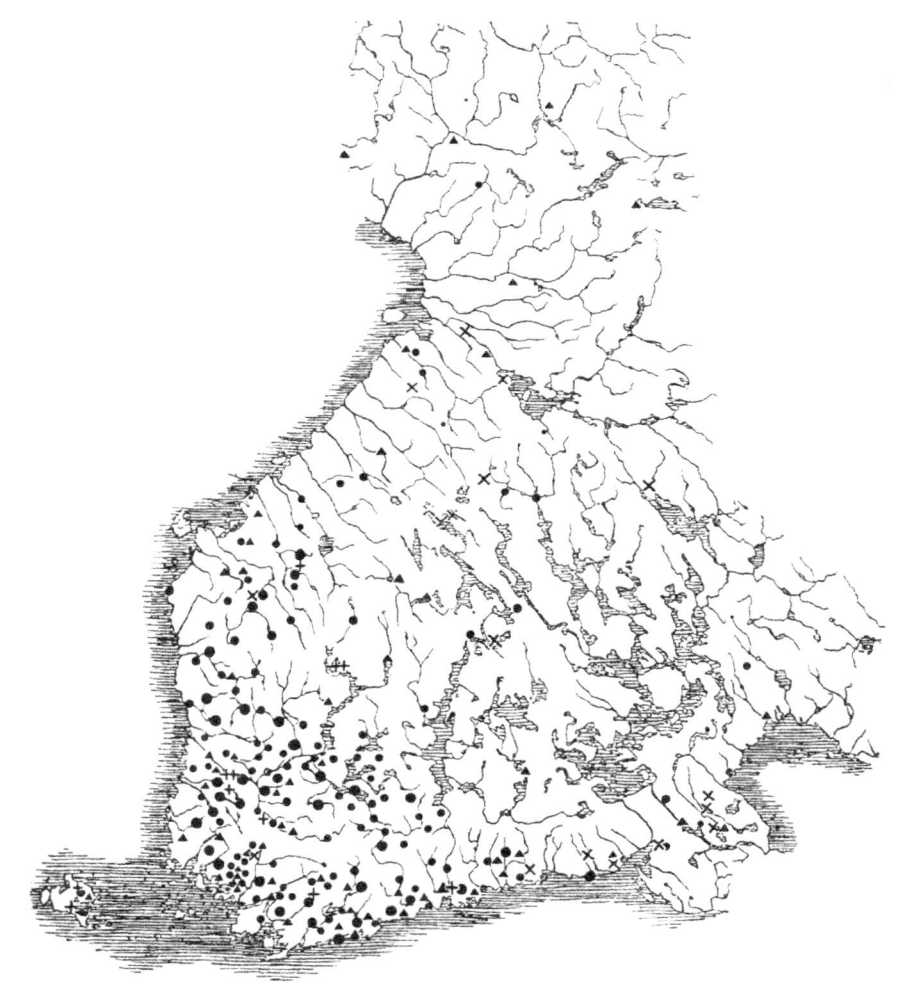

Fig. 120: Map of the distribution of sites with comb ceramics (✕), other pottery (+), "Swedish" battle axes (▲), and Pre-Finnic boat axes (●) in Finland (per Almgren).

component of the central Russian Fatyanovo civilization was still evident in their preference for sculpted animal motifs on battle axes and daggers (Figs. 134, 135), in both stone and copper, whereby the moose head motif still played the same role as it had, in conjunction with the bear head and the dog head, further northward in both northern Russia and eastern Finland.

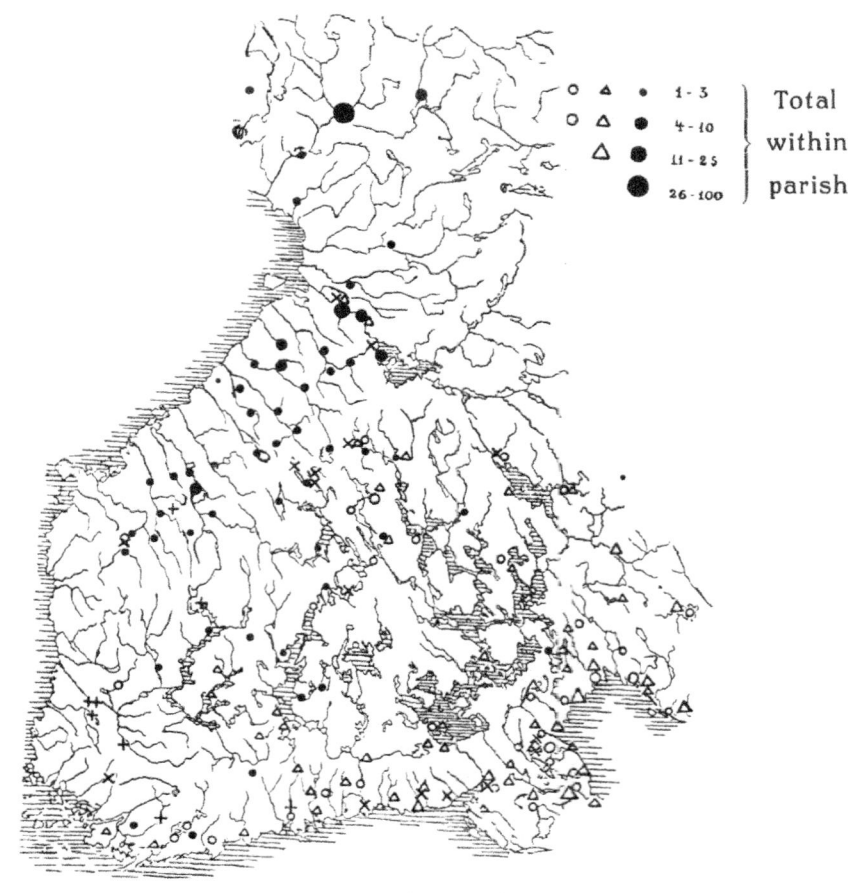

Fig. 121: Map of the distribution of "cradle-shaped" pickaxes such as in Fig. 95 (○), "Russian Karelian" chisels such as in Fig. 93 (△), Rovaniemi pickaxes such as in Fig. 94 (●), comb ceramics (×), and other ceramics (+) in Finland (per Almgren).

Fig. 122a: Saarijärvi, Tavastia. Sled runner with a length of 2.21m.
(The pegs inserted into the initially empty holes are new).

Fig. 122b: Section of the sled runner in Fig. 122a.
(per A. Europäus and S. Pälsi.)

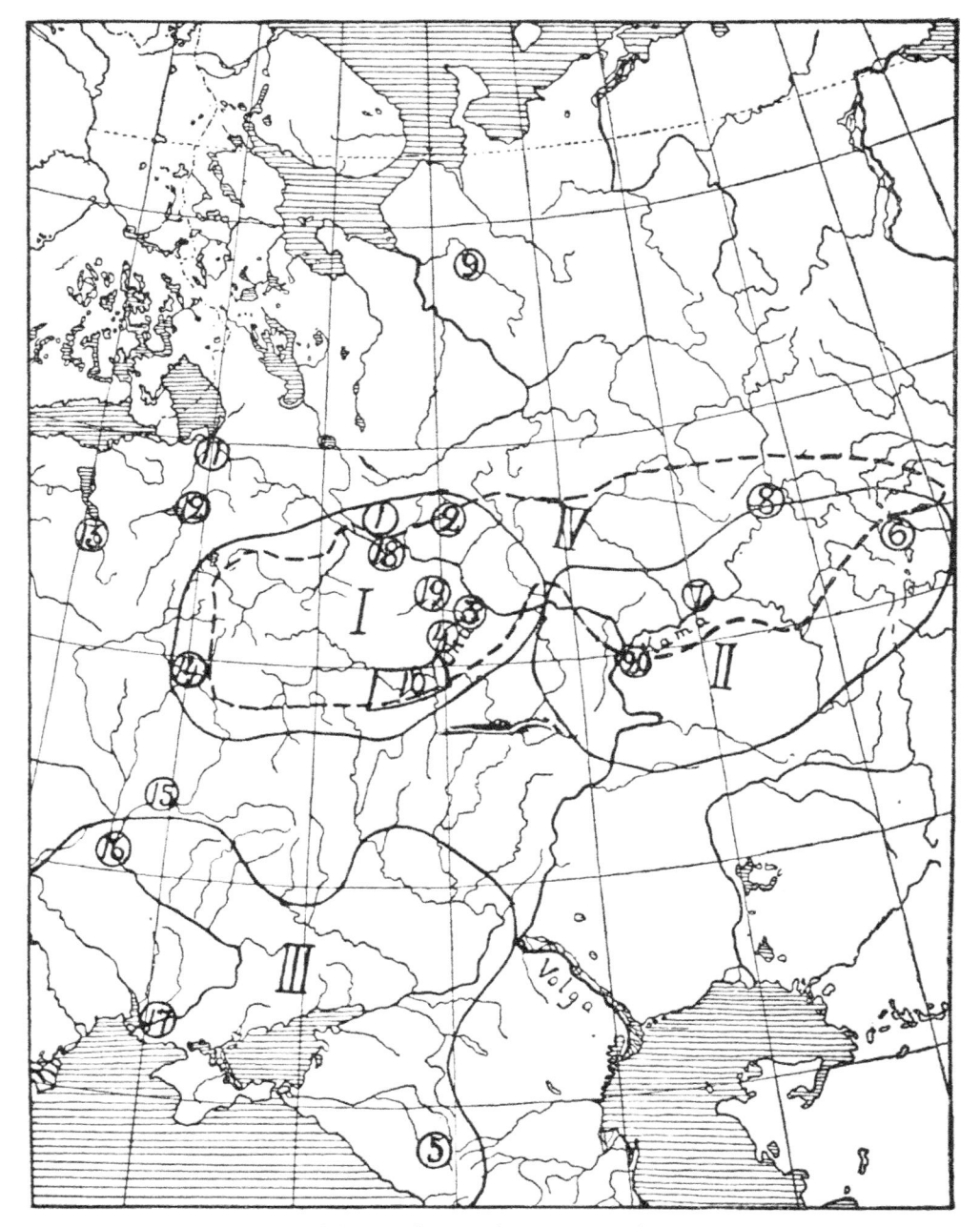

Fig. 123: Map of the distribution of Stone Age civilizations in Russia.
I. Fatyanovo civilization. II. Copper civilization of eastern Russia. III. Area of the large kurgans in southern Russia. -------- Area of the Gorodishche.
1. Fatyanovo; 2. Galich; 4. Seima; 4. Volosovo (Vladimir governorate); 18. Velikoye Selo (Yaroslavl governorate); 19. Churkina (Nizhny Novgorod governorate); 10. Dubrovichi (Ryazan governorate); 14. Dyadkovichi and Brassovo (Oryol governorate); 16. Jackovica (Kiev governorate); 17. Belozerka (Kherson governorate); 5. Maykop.

Finally, from the archeological site near Volosovo, Vladimir governorate, we shall not neglect to mention the strange human and animal figurines[1] carved in flint (Figs. 136–139). They are reminiscent of the similar flat bone carvings with human and animal designs (Figs. 140, 141) that have been discovered at the Stone Age settlement on the southern shore of Lake Ladoga[2].

In contrast to both this basal component and its superimposed Central European overlay is the content of metal

Fig. 124: Nova Syniava (Podolia).

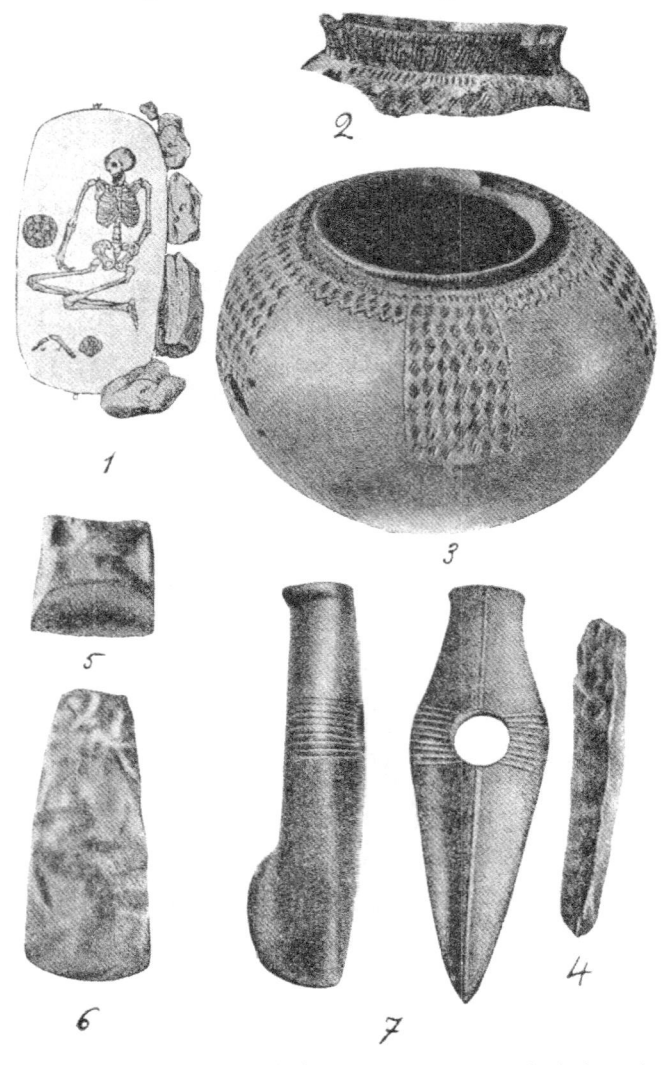

Fig. 125: Fatyanovo (Yaroslavl governorate): Typical finds from the burial grounds (per A. M. Tallgren).
1. Single earth grave from Velikoye Selo; 2., 3. Clay vessels;
4.–6. Flint implements (scraper, chisel, axe); 7. Boat axe.

---

[1] P. Koudriavtsev: *Congrès international d'archéologie et d'anthropologie préhistoriques* XI. Moscou 1892, Vol. II, pp. 247 ff. and Aleksey Uvarov: *Archeologija Rossii, Kamennij Period* Vol. II, Moscow 1881 (Russian); Plate 31.

[2] See: Otto Tischler: "Die neuesten Entdeckungen aus der Steinzeit im ostbaltischen Gebiet und die Anfänge der plastischen Kunst in Nordost-Europa" (*Schriften der Physikalisch-Ökonomischen Gesellschaft zu Königsberg* 1883. XXIV, pp. 96 f.); see also the previously cited work by Inostrantsev, p. 48, Footnote 2.

implements, which appear sparsely in the burial grounds, but are very abundant in two corresponding finds of treasure hoards, one from Galich, Kostroma governorate, and one from Seima, Nizhny Novgorod governorate. Among these,

Fig. 126: ¹/₃. Eastern Russia, Copper boat axe (per Tallgren).

Fig. 127: Jackowica (County Lipovets, Kiev governorate): Tumulus 29 (*Mannus* II).

Figs. 128, 129: Jackowica (County Lipovets, Kiev governorate). (*Mannus* II).

Figs. 130–132: Jackowica (County Lipovets, Kiev governorate). (*Mannus* II).

the leading roles are played by copper flat daggers (Fig. 134), copper knives, copper jewelry (rings, pendants, beads) and, in particular, copper battle axes, the shaft hole of which is located all the way at the rear of the sharply angled butt, and of which about eight were found in total (Fig. 142): one special type (type A per Tallgren) of these copper axes which have been found in such vast quantities from Hungary to the Caucasus and even further afield to Turkestan, and which is most widespread in central-eastern Russia, also made its way from there to the interior of the Fatyanovo civilization of central Russia.

Fig. 133: Kobrynova and Ryzhanovka near Zvenigorodka (Kiev governorate). (*Mannus* II.)

Fig. 135: Seima: Dagger pommel; compare with Fig. 125 (per Tallgren).

Fig. 134: Seima, Nizhny Novgorod governorate: Copper dagger with moose head pommel.

These copper objects, along with a few silver beads and a bronze ingot, testify to a noticeable influence of the Kuban civilization of southeastern Russia (Fig. 123, III). However, this southern influence was by no means strong enough to be regarded as decisive for the ethnic allocation of the Fatyanovo civilization as a whole. Rather, its primary characteristics were Northern Indo-Germanic, whereas the Kuban civilization was undoubtedly an extension of the Danubian civilization of the Southern Indo-Germanic Satem tribes. I therefore cannot agree with Tallgren's view that the Fatyanovo civilization, whose Indo-Germanic character Tallgren maintains with certainty on the basis of my account,[1] was Southern Indo-Germanic and that its disappearance at the end of the Stone Age signified an emigration of the Indo-Germanic peoples from there to the Caucasus as well as to Persia. Rather, the demise of the Fatyanovo civilization should be viewed in relation to the termination of settlement at the end of the entire third wave of Northern Indo-Germanic migration to southern Russia, which I have called the Corded Ware migration.

Where these Northern Indo-Germanics, including the Fatyanovo population, moved on to from southern and inner Russia cannot yet be determined

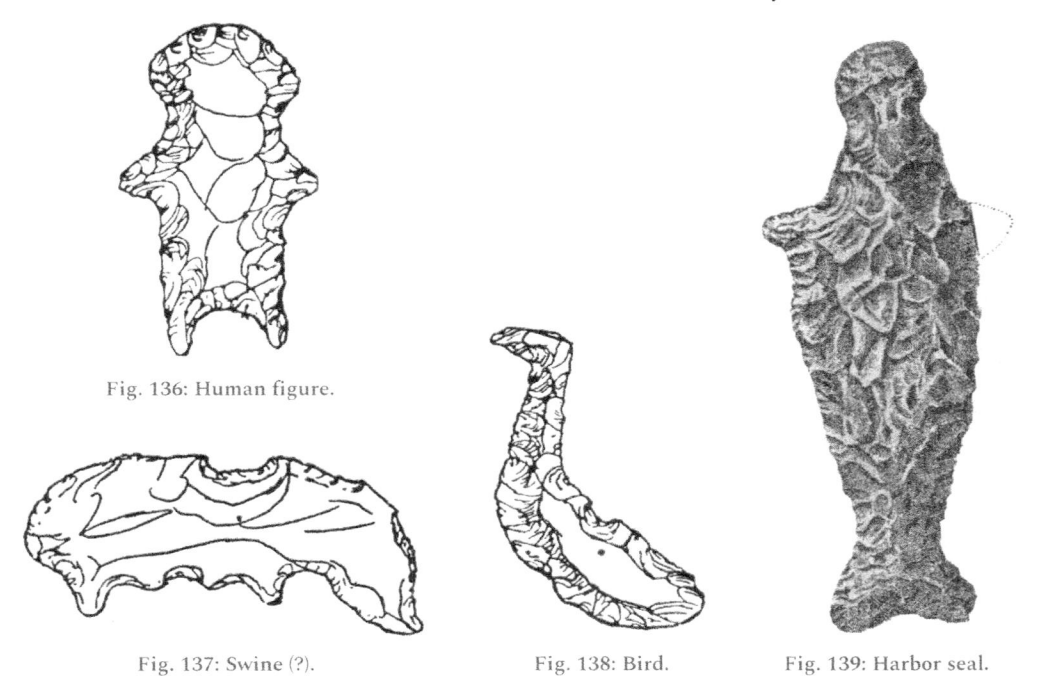

Fig. 136: Human figure.

Fig. 137: Swine (?).   Fig. 138: Bird.   Fig. 139: Harbor seal.

Figs. 136–139: Volosovo, Vladimir governorate: Amulets made of flint.

archaeologically. The only ethnic group in Asia known to have had a Northern Indo-Germanic language are the Hittites[2]. The Tocharians, who were long thought to also have been Northern Indo-Germanics, have turned out, thanks to Pokorny's penetrating examination of their language, to have been a segment of

---

[1] *Mannus* II. 1910.
[2] Friedrich Hrozny: *Die Sprache der Hethiter*. Leipzig 1917. (Otto Weber's *Boghazköi-Studien*, H. 1, 2); see also: *Mitteilungen der Deutschen Orient Gesellschaft* No. 56 (Dec. 1915).

the Thracian-Phrygian language group that had branched off very early[1]. From a linguistic point of view, one could therefore conjecture that the Northern Indo-Germanics of southern Russia could have gone on to form the Indo-Germanic component of the later Hittite or Kanesian people, who crossed the Caucasus and merged with the sub-population of the Luwians in eastern Asia Minor to form the unified Kanesian people with the Kanesian language, named after the capital of Kanes (Boğazköy) near Ancyra. Yet the pre-Hittite Luwians were not themselves the indigenous population of Asia Minor. That would rather have been the Hattians proper (Proto-Hattians = Proto-Hittites), a Caucasian tribe, while the Luwians are thought to have been a southern branch of the Finno-Ugrians due to very striking linguistic similarities, in part with Indo-Germanic and in part with Finnic[2]. One could therefore associate the Luwians with the Fatyanovo population and the still-unmixed Hittites with the pure Northern Indo-Germanics of the third wave of migration to southern

Figs. 140, 141: Lake Ladoga shoreline: Bone carvings; man and harbor seal.

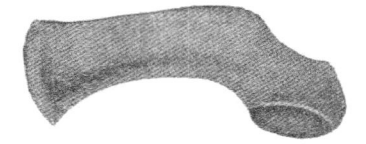

Fig. 142: Galich, Kostroma governorate: Copper axe.

Russia. The fact that the Hittite-Kanesians of Asia Minor appear to have been the enemies of a king of the Akkadian dynasty, who most probably was Naram-Sin, in other words, what could have been as early as around 2750 BC, is not an insurmountable obstacle to such a conjecture. For there is no doubt in my mind that Tallgren's dating of the Fatyanovo civilization to 2000 BC falls a great

---

[1] Julius Pokorny: "Die Stellung des Tocharischen im Kreise der indogermanischen Sprachen" (*Berichte des Forschungs-Instituts für Osten und Orient in Wien* Bd. III, 1919).

[2] Emil Forrer ("Die acht Sprachen der Boghazköi-Inschriften": *Sitzungsberichte der Preussischen Akademie der Wissenschaften* 1919, Bd. II, pp. 1029 ff.) mentions such similarities: Reduplication in the past tense, pronouns *kui, kuis,* etc., possessive suffix *-mis, -tis, -tis* (such as in Luwian and Kanesian), verbal endings *-du, -andu, -indu* (as in Lydian).

number of centuries too late[1].

In any event, the segment of the "Pre-Finns" that was absorbed into the Fatyanovo population could hardly have had anything to do with the adoption of Indo-Iranic loanwords into Finno-Ugric as a whole.

That role was more likely to have been played by the population of the Copper civilization of eastern Russia, whose territory was situated directly adjacent to the

Fig. 143: ⅓. Magdeburg. Provincial Museum Halle. H. K. 3554.
This image is courtesy of the Museum Halle.

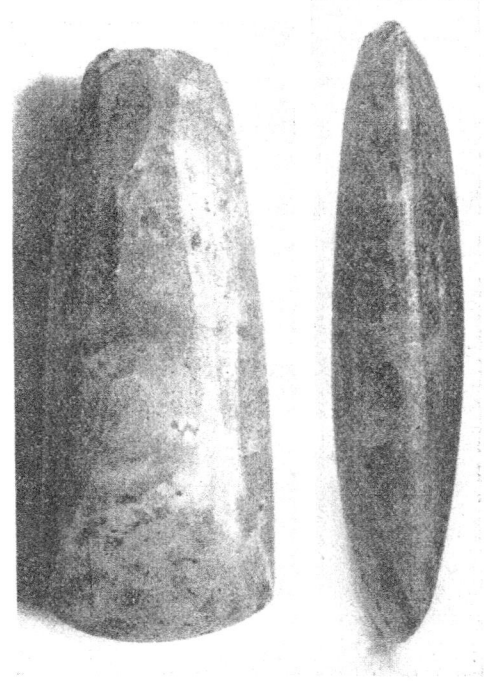

Fig. 144: ⅓. Grenzau, Kreis Unterwesterwald, Nassau. Provincial Museum Bonn 1670.

eastern border of the Fatyanovo area on the middle Volga (near Kazan) and on the river Kama, and which is labeled II on our map (Fig. 123). This territory encompassed the governorates of Nizhny Novgorod, Kazan, Simbirsk, Vyatka, Perm, and Ufa. This region occupies a somewhat special position insofar as its numerous Stone Age find sites also contain the pottery that we characterized in preceding pages as "East Finnic," yet here these ceramic vessels were always flat-

---

[1] Even more grievous is Tallgren's miscalculation concerning the civilization of the inland Jutlanders of the earliest Boat Axe period and the Passage Grave period, which he also wants to date to around 2000 BC, that is, to the end of the Nordic Stone Cist period or right in the middle of Period I of the Central European Bronze Age.

bottomed. There is an extremely rich supply of sometimes very well-crafted flintwork, flint knives (an influence of the Fatyanovo civilization), and solid rock implements, as well as perforated marble balls (club heads?); scarcer here are boat axes. In addition, there were a large number of copper implements that had been imported from southern Russia or Transylvania, some of which were replicated in Uralic copper, such as flat axes, flat daggers (around 100 pieces), battle axes of type A with shaft-holed butts (see again Fig. 142; also around 100 pieces), crescent-shaped chisels, and triangular flat arrowheads[1]. Here we first of all have an almost exclusively southern influence on this otherwise unaltered native civilization. And secondly, this civilization continued without interruption throughout the Bronze Age and into the early Iron Age, which began here around 600 BC (Ananyino period)[2], and then continued through the so-called civilization of Pianobor (situated on the Kama) from the first centuries of our calendar until around 600 AD, whereas the Fatyanovo civilization in Region I of our map had come to a halt without any further continuation[3].

During the earliest Iron Age, triangular ramparts with exceptionally meager civilizational content, which we now call *gorodishche*, were built on plateaus along the angle of confluence of two rivers. These fortified settlements not only covered the eastern Russian Bronze area in question, but they were also spread across the former Fatyanovo territory in inner Russia, which had previously been so long-deserted (see map: Fig. 123). It was therefore probably the Copper and Bronze areas of eastern Russia which, while remaining purely Finno-Ugric, received the Indo-Iranic and very shortly thereafter the purely Iranic influence from the Caucasus whereby it was then imparted to all Finno-Ugrians. The westward expansion of this area during the Gorodishche period could perhaps have introduced the Baltic-Lithuanian civilizational influence throughout the West Finns and the Volga Finns, whereas a short while later the West Finns alone became exposed to the flow of Scandinavian-Germanic civilization and culture. Of course, we cannot archaeologically establish the Germanic influence upon

---

[1] For more on the Copper and Bronze areas of eastern Russia, see Tallgren: *Kupfer- und Bronzezeit* pp. 105-136, and especially Tallgren: *Collection Zaoussailov*. Helsingfors 1916.

[2] Tallgren: *L'époque dite d'Ananino*. Helsingfors 1919; Tallgren (p. 184) thinks the civilization of Ananyino (Vyatka governorate) represents the Magyars of that time, that is, the Ugric branch of the Finno-Ugrians.

[3] Only from the aforementioned site of Seima (Nizhny-Novgorod governorate) do we have a find from Period II of the Bronze Age, in other words from around 1600 BC, which therefore does not establish any cultural connection either forwards or backwards in time; see Tallgren: "Den äldsta ostryska Bronsaldern": *Rig*, Vol. II/III 1919/20, pp. 65 ff.

Finland, nor upon the Baltic lands, during the pre-Christian Iron Age, as Finland around that time was almost completely devoid of settlements. The earliest recognizable Germanic influences only appear in the 2nd century AD and did not penetrate into Finland by way of Sweden, but rather by way of Estonia[1].

4. The First Cleavage of the Proto-Indo-Germanics

Even more important for the Indo-Germanic question than the emergence and dispersal of those Pre-Finns who had managed to retain their independence are the developments concerning the segment of the Dobbertin population that was unable to escape the grasp of the Indo-Germanics: here a mixture which I call the Finno-Indo-Germanics emerged. In southeastern Sweden we have already become acquainted with the bearers of the Boat Axe Civilization. In inland Jutland and inland Schleswig-Holstein, the even more significant major western branch of the Finno-Indo-Germanic people arose. More on them in a moment.

With the creation of the point-butted flint axe (Fig. 59), the Early Neolithic or Middle Stone Age period came to an end. This was followed by the marked progression to the thin-butted flint axe (Fig. 143), which was found only in very exceptional cases in the latest, uppermost cultural layer of the period of the earlier shell middens, and still only quite seldomly in that of the later shell middens. In the main, these axes belonged to the beginning of the later Late Neolithic Stone Age, the period of the large stone tombs, which must have begun around 4000 BC. I have become ever more convinced that the concept of the stone tomb spread from Portugal to Ireland and from there onwards to Denmark. Brittany presents the best case as a by no means certain conduit through which the concept could have instead spread out of France, unless, as seems more likely to me, this peninsula first received the inspiration for the construction of stone tombs from Ireland and from there passed it on in a broad diagonal southeastward stroke to southeastern France (see the map on p. 90). However, I reject any notion of a simultaneous migration of the Megalithic population along the aforementioned route towards the Baltic Sea to any significant extent, because the spreading of the construction of stone tombs was not accompanied in the slightest by a simultaneous spreading of the cultural content that had been associated with the stone tombs of Western Europe. Rather, at the beginning of the Stone Tomb period, trade and traffic between the flint civilization on the Baltic Sea and its

---

[1] A. Hackman: *Mannus* V. 1913. pp. 282 ff and pp. 293 ff.

colonial territories in Western Europe ceased (pp. 31 f.). The fully developed form of the Nordic thin-butted axe (Fig. 143) was no longer attained in Western Europe: the artfully hewn narrow edges were missing here, such that the cross-section of the axe remained oval-edged or became faintly oval-edged, that is, it had rounded edges, or in very rare cases slight, but still irregular narrow edges, which were never artfully hewn, as in the North, but crudely polished (Fig. 144). And the development of the flint axe in Western Europe, whether in France or in England, remained at this level until the end of the Stone Age, aside from the gradual and ever-increasing degeneration of this form. — (See Supplements pp. 82 f.)

A map of the distribution of the thin-butted flint axe shows that the western and southern boundaries of the authentically Nordic form of this tool ran from the southeastern shore of the Zuiderzee through Münster and Osnabrück and onward to the northern slopes of the Harz and then northward from there through

Fig. 145: Duchy of Schleswig. Museum Kiel.

Fig. 146: Vedbøl, Haderslev Municipality. Museum Haderslev.

Figs. 145, 146: ⅓. Funnel beakers of the Dolmen Period, some with vertical furrows, some with vertical ridges.

Halberstadt to Magdeburg and onward to Stendal. To the east of the Elbe, in addition to the Nordic countries and Schleswig-Holstein, it also covered Mecklenburg, Rügen, Western Pomerania, the Uckermark, and the western half of Eastern Pomerania. On the other hand, the western type of thin-butted flint axe began to acutely emerge from near Münster and the Zuiderzee and from here it spread westward and southwestward across the Lower Rhine and Belgium into northeastern France along the aforementioned broad wedge-shaped area. As a result of the rise of agriculture among the descendants of those Ellerbek people that had remained in their Baltic Sea homeland, they penetrated further into the interior of their homeland, that is, into northern Germany, and were no longer compelled to emigrate to Western Europe. The resulting interruption of traffic to Western Europe from the quantitatively and qualitatively far superior Nordic hearth of flint technology led to a withering of the progress of the Western European offshoots, while the main branch, the Proto-Indo-Germanics on the Baltic Sea, continued flourishing with full vigor and vitality. It was these later Ellerbekers of the Baltic Sea coasts, that is, the Proto-Indo-Germanics, and only

Fig. 147: Vedbøl, Haderslev Municipality. Museum Haderslev.

Fig. 148: Ohlsdorf, Eppendorf parish, Holstein. Museum Hamburg.

Figs. 147, 148: $^1/_3$. Collared flasks from the Dolmen Period.

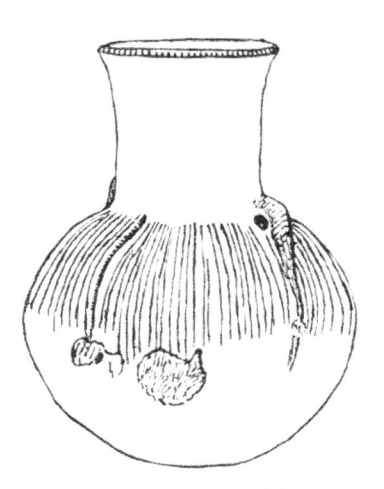

Fig. 149: Northern Schleswig. Museum Copenhagen.

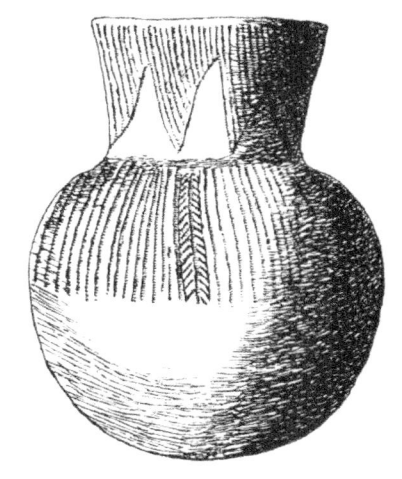

Fig. 150: Stenvad, Randers Municipality, Jutland.

Fig. 149, 150: $^1/_4$. Globular flasks from the Dolmen Period.

these, and not the inland population, who adopted and implemented the concept of the stone tombs.

Concurrent with the earliest coastal and island dolmens, we see a rejection of the stone tomb with its crowded inhumations and instead a persistence of the more ancient single earth grave throughout the whole of Inner Jutland, even though the Indo-Germanic influence had also initially dominated in Inner Jutland during this earliest period of stone tombs. This can be seen through their adoption of the entire material culture of the Dolmen civilization, that is, the pottery, which consisted of the three vessel types of the funnel beaker (Figs. 145, 146), the collared flask (Figs. 147, 148) and the globular flask (Figs. 149, 150), all three still fashioned in their earliest forms with rounded bottoms, as well as the thin-butted flint axe (Fig. 143), and finally, the clubs made of solid rock and the amber jewelry. The situation became quite different during the subsequent Passage Grave period, when the ancient Dobbertiners of inland Jutland triumphantly re-emerged from the slight inundation of the Indo-Germanic Dolmen civilization as a special new people, an independent Finno-Indo-Germanic tribe, a topic which shall be covered in Part Two of this book.

It was during the period of the ancient dolmens that we must mark the beginning of a civilization that was as uniform across its many directions as it was sharply divergent from the Baltic Sea civilization; this civilization, which I once collectively designated the Danubian civilization and attributed to the "Southern Indo-Germanics," was ancestral to the later Eastern Indo-Germanics, while during this same period the Indo-Germanics of the original Baltic Sea homeland became the Northern Indo-Germanics, who were the ancestors of the later Western Indo-Germanics. Alas, it has not yet been possible to find an archaeological connection between these Northern and Southern Indo-Germanic cultures in such a way that would demonstrate the separation of the latter from the former at a rupture point or connective seam. This is a painful gap in our understanding of the archaeological material. We must assume that the primeval forest that covered Central Europe in the Early Neolithic period, with the exception of the coastal regions and perhaps the banks of the larger rivers[1], had already contracted enough by the Dolmen period as a result of the onset of the warmer and drier climate that prevailed throughout the entire Neolithic and the Bronze Age that the Indo-Germanic Baltic Sea population of the time was able to send significant components across the Central European interior and into the regions of the middle Danube without difficulty. For it is there, with the extensive loess areas on the Hungarian Danube-Tisza plain as its central hub, that we must

---

[1] Ernst Wahle: "Deutschland zur jüngeren Steinzeit" (Special printing from: *Zwölf länderkundliche Studien. Von Schülern Alfred Hettners ihrem Lehrer zum 60. Geburtstage*. Breslau 1921, pp. 9 ff.) pp. 13 ff.

seek the first roots and settlements of the Danubian civilization: it is there that we find its earliest, most primitive manifestations, its densest settlements, its richest developments, and later its strongest influences upon the Upper Danube and the Middle Rhine[1].

With the emergence of this second civilization, the Danubian civilization, which was so vastly divergent from the Nordic civilization both geographically and in terms of content, the unity of the Proto-Indo-Germanics was dissolved. However, the two civilizations soon coalesced, at least geographically. And thus began the period of common Indo-Germanic, which was marked by the long struggle for supremacy between smaller or larger tribal offshoots, especially among the Northern Indo-Germanics — just like at the beginning of the time of the Germanic Völkerwanderung — and which ended with the formation of the various independent Indo-Germanic peoples and the conquest of Southern Europe by the Northern Indo-Germanics and of the Near East by the Southern Indo-Germanics. All of this will be addressed in Part Two of this outline.

---

[1] *Mannus* I, pp. 233 ff.

Table.

Period	Years Before Christ	Schleswig-Holstein, Jutland	Danish Islands	
Early Iron Age	Around Christ's birth to 750 BC	Ingvaeones	Funen: Ingvaeones; Zealand: North Germanics	1.
Bronze Age V – Ic	750—1900	Germanics	Germanics	2.
a) Neolithic Stone Cists; b) Single Earth Graves	1900—2400		Beginning of (Amalgamation Indo-Germanics and	3.
a) Later Passage Graves; b) Single Earth Graves	2400—2800 (?)	a) East coast and north: North Indo-Germanics; b) Inland and west coast: Finno-Indo-Germanics	Northern Indo-Germanics (only sporadically: Finno-Indo-Germanics)	4.
a) Earlier Passage Graves; b) Single Earth Graves (thick-butted axe)	2800—3200 (?)	a) East coast and north: North Indo-Germanics; b) Inland and west coast: Finno-Indo-Germanics	Northern Indo-Germanics	5.
a) Dolmen; b) Single Earth Graves (thin-butted axe)	3200—4000 (?)	a) East coast and north coast: North Indo-Germanics; b) Inland and west coast: Finno-Indo-Germanics	Northern Indo-Germanics	6.
Later Shell Midden (point-butted axe)	3500—4500 (?)	a) Proto-Indo-Germanics b) Post-Ice-Age proto-folk	a) Proto-Indo-Germanics; b) Post-Ice-Age proto-folk	7.
Earlier Shell Midden (core axe, cleaver) Littorina stage	4500—6000 (?)	a) Pre-Indo-Germanics b) Post-Ice-Age proto-folk		8.
Ancylus stage (Bone Period)	6000—10000	sparsely populated	heavily populated	9.
		Post-Ice-Age proto-folk		
Yoldia stage	10000—12000	Post-Ice-Age proto-folk		10.
Magdalénian	12000—15000	glaciated		11.

Table.

	Southern Scandinavia up to the Dal River	Northern Scandinavia	Finland	East-Russia
1.	North Germanics	Proto-Lapps Proto-Finns	Proto-Lapps Proto-Finns	Gorodishche Ananyino
2.	Germanics	Pre-Finns	Southwest: Germanics	settlements
3.	the Germanics of Northern Finno-Indo-Germanics)	Pre-Finns	vacant	settlements
4.	a) West coast: Northern Indo-Germanics; b) East coast: Finno-Indo-Germanics (Boat Axe civilization)	Pre-Finns (later "Arctic" civilization)	a) Southwest: Northern Indo-Germanics; b) North and east: Pre-Finns	East and central: Copper and Fatyanovo civilization
5.	a) West coast: Northern Indo-Germanics; b) East coast: Pre-Finns (Dwelling-Place civilization)	vacant	vacant	?
6.	a) West coast: Northern Indo-Germanics; b) East coast and south coast: Pre-Finns (later round-butted axe)	vacant	vacant	?
7.	a) Scania: Proto-Indo-Germanics; b) Central and north: Proto-folk (earlier round-butted axe)	vacant	vacant	?
8.	a) South: Pre-Indo-Germanics; b) Central and north: Post-Ice-Age proto-folk (Nöstvet-Lihult-round-butted axe civilization)	vacant	vacant	in Lithuania, Volhynia, Podolia: traces of settlement
9.	Post-Ice-Age proto-folk	still glaciated	Post-Ice-Age proto-folk	?
10.	All glaciated except Scania		partly glaciated, partly under sea	?
11.	glaciated			?

Supplements

1.

On p. 4, Footnote 6: I could also have mentioned here the presence of two pond turtle plastrons in the newly discovered dwelling-place of the earliest Dobbertiner population in Svärdborg Bog (see Footnote 3 on p. 20) which were documented by Friis Johansen (*Aarbøger for nordisk Oldkyndighed og Historie*. 1919, p. 128).

2.

On p. 26: In *Rogalands Stenalder* (Stavanger 1920) pp. 151 ff., a work that I received during my proofreading for this work, Helge Gjessing has demonstrated through a thorough evaluation of the finds from an archaeological standpoint that the site of Viste in Randaberg parish, Hetland municipality, district of Jæderen did not belong to the Early Neolithic period, but to the beginning of the Late Neolithic period (Dolmen period). The remnants of polished stone axes from the bottommost layers of the dig site show that the few older forms of implements that have been discovered there owe their long-enduring invariability to the strictly conservative character of the Pre-Finnic fisher population. — Incidentally, the accuracy of the equally early dating of the Kunda find site in Estonia has also been disputed; see M. Ebert: *Prähistorische Zeitschrift* V 1913, p. 507. It will therefore be necessary to look for another, more reliably dated find site whose name could be used to designate the later phase of the civilization of the Ancylus stage (that of the Dobbertin population).

3.

On p. 55: For more on the rock carvings and rock paintings of an Arctic character in southern Norway, see also Jan Petersen: *Naturen* 1917, pp. 134 ff. and pp. 178 ff., as well as H. Gjessing, *op. cit.* pp. 170 ff.

4.

On pp. 75–76: With a few brief remarks I shall return to the question of whether it can be assumed that the construction of the megalithic tombs, if indeed, as I believe, it did spread into the Baltic Rim by way of Ireland, was facilitated by a significant emigration of Irish or even British populations. I reject this assumption because we know extraordinarily little about the civilization of this British population, since the megalithic tombs there are only very sparsely furnished with grave goods, and in any case, we have not detected even the slightest intrusion of British civilizational influences into the Baltic region. Therefore, when Knut Stjerna derived the population and civilization of the Scandinavian megalithic tombs directly from Great Britain, it seems to me that this was just yet another of his rash conclusions.

It is therefore regrettable that the excellent anthropological researcher Carl M. Fürst, in his reconstruction of the history of the Scandinavian Stone Age population from an anthropological point of view, was completely under the spell of Stjernian ideas. Fürst, like me in 1908, although unaware of my publication in *Mannus* I, conjectured[1] that the Early Neolithic population of the Nordic countries could have belonged to a purely short-headed race (although he had no knowledge of any Early Neolithic skulls at all) and that a purely long-skulled race would only have arrived in conjunction with the Megalithic civilization from Britain. This emigration would have purportedly involved such vast numbers and such success in terms of domination that this new population in Scandinavia would have represented the race we now know as the Nordic long-headed race.

The primary anthropological reason for Fürst's assumption was his belief that both the British as well as the Swedish long-skulled Megalithic populations were of short stature: long bones were found in the dolmen of Slutarp in Västergötland, from which Fürst calculated a height of 145–168 cm for men and 147–162 cm for women. I shall not presume to judge the extent to which such mere extrapolations deserve to be trusted. However, one becomes perplexed when he considers that Nielsen calculated an average height of 170 cm for men and 155 cm for women for the Danish Stone Age population, that is, figures that were extraordinarily higher than those given by Fürst for Sweden. That said, these figures of Nielsen's only applied to the long-skulled segment of the Danish Megalithic population, while the short-skulled segment was shorter. Yet what shall we make of the fact that back in his day Gustaf Retzius had estimated the average height of Swedish Stone Age people at 167 cm (as opposed to 171 cm in the present day)? Surely Fürst's figures are far too incongruent with those.

In sum, I have seen nothing in anthropology or archaeology that could induce me to depart in any way from my views on the races as I have developed them within this book.

---

[1] Carl M. Fürst: *Die Kraniologie der schwedischen Steinzeit*, p. 63; Fürst: *Neolithische Schädel von der Insel Ösel* (1914), p. 43.

— 84 —

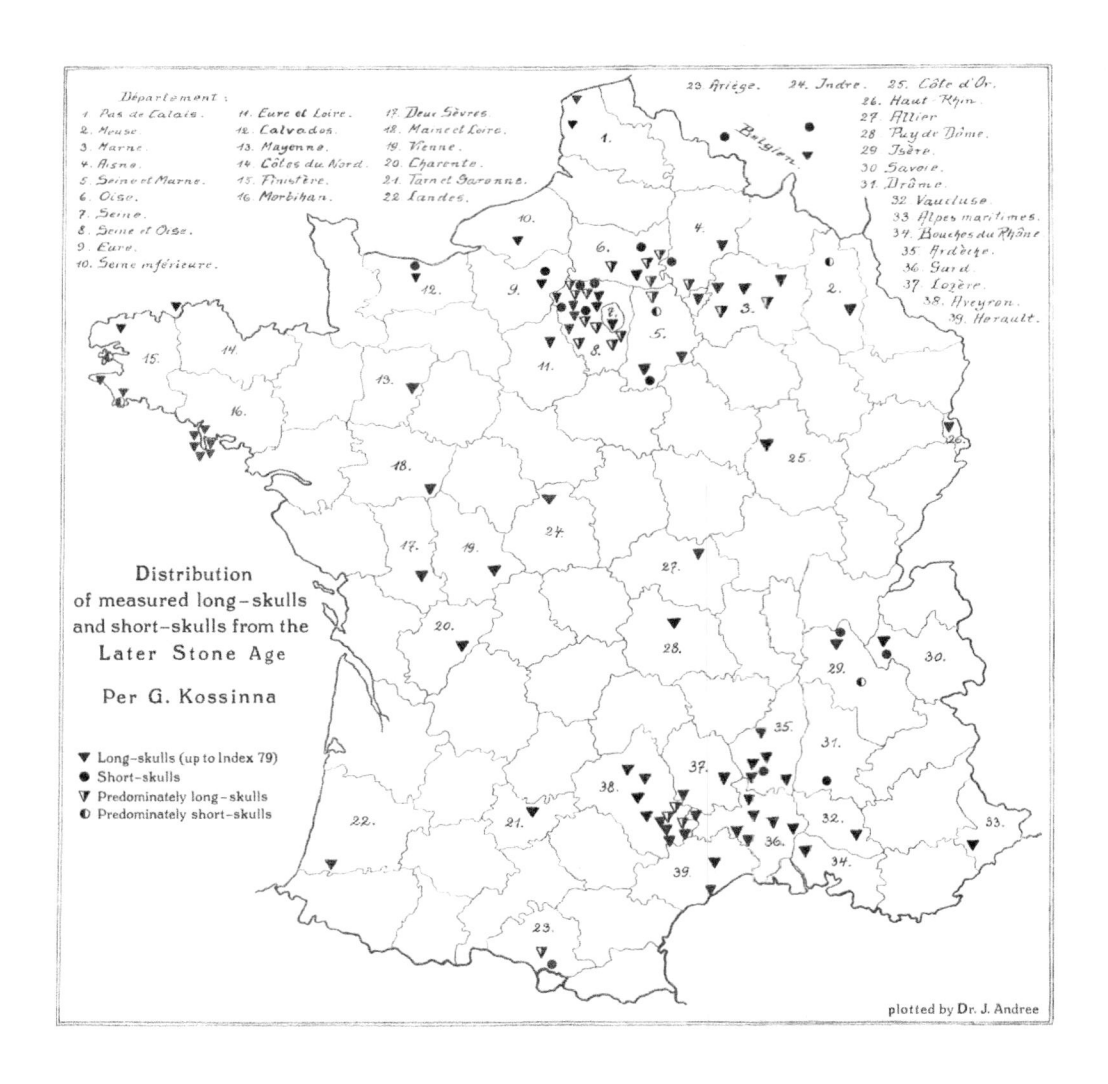

Distribution of measured long-skulls and short-skulls from the Later Stone Age

Per G. Kossinna

▼ Long-skulls (up to Index 79)
● Short-skulls
▽ Predominately long-skulls
◐ Predominately short-skulls

Département:
1. Pas de Calais
2. Meuse
3. Marne
4. Aisne
5. Seine et Marne
6. Oise
7. Seine
8. Seine et Oise
9. Eure
10. Seine inférieure
11. Eure et Loire
12. Calvados
13. Mayenne
14. Côtes du Nord
15. Finistère
16. Morbihan
17. Deux Sèvres
18. Maine et Loire
19. Vienne
20. Charente
21. Tarn et Garonne
22. Landes
23. Ariège
24. Indre
25. Côte d'Or
26. Haut-Rhin
27. Allier
28. Puy de Dôme
29. Isère
30. Savoie
31. Drôme
32. Vaucluse
33. Alpes maritimes
34. Bouches du Rhône
35. Ardèche
36. Gard
37. Lozère
38. Aveyron
39. Hérault

plotted by Dr. J. Andree

(Per K. Keilhack).

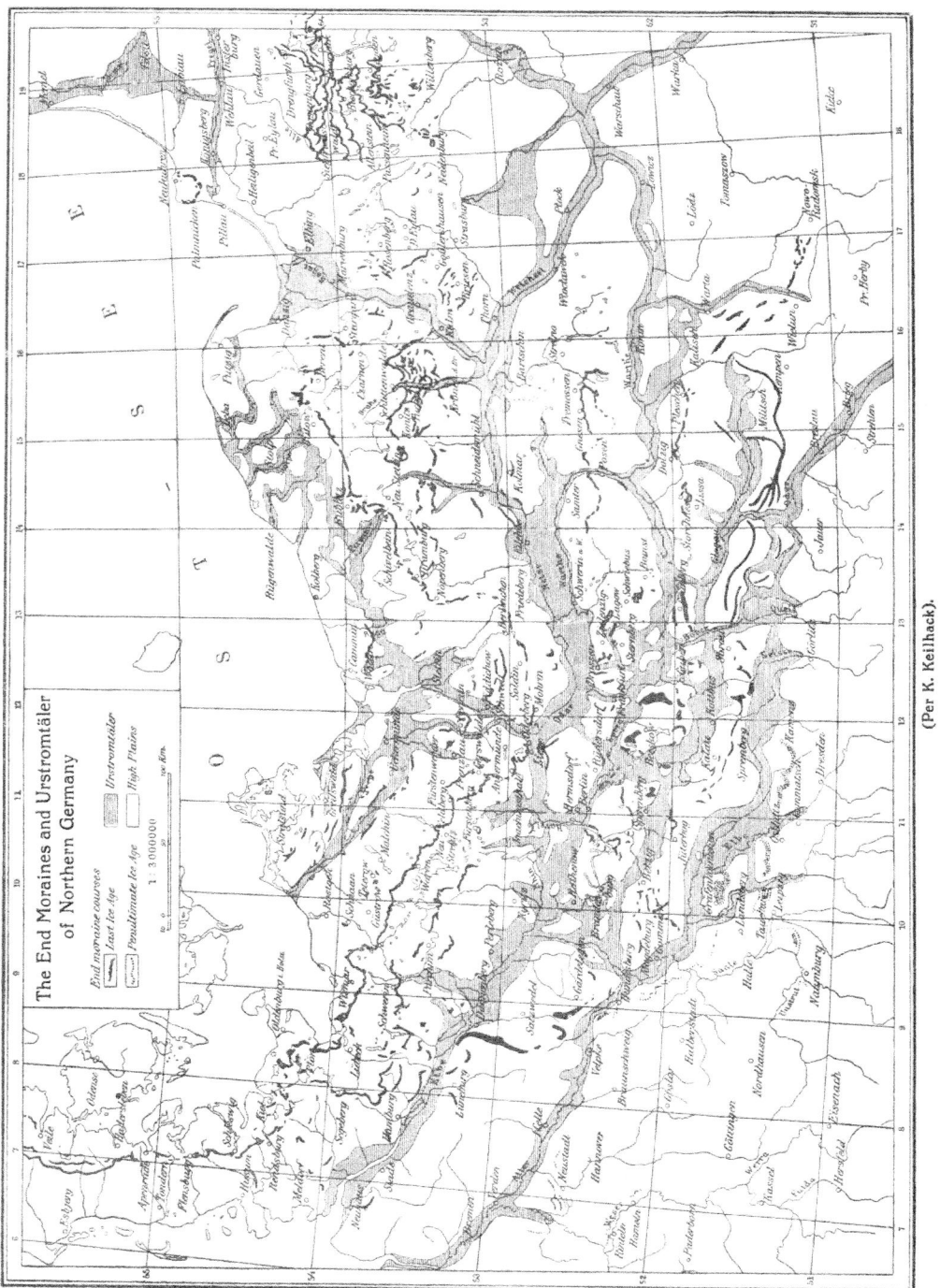

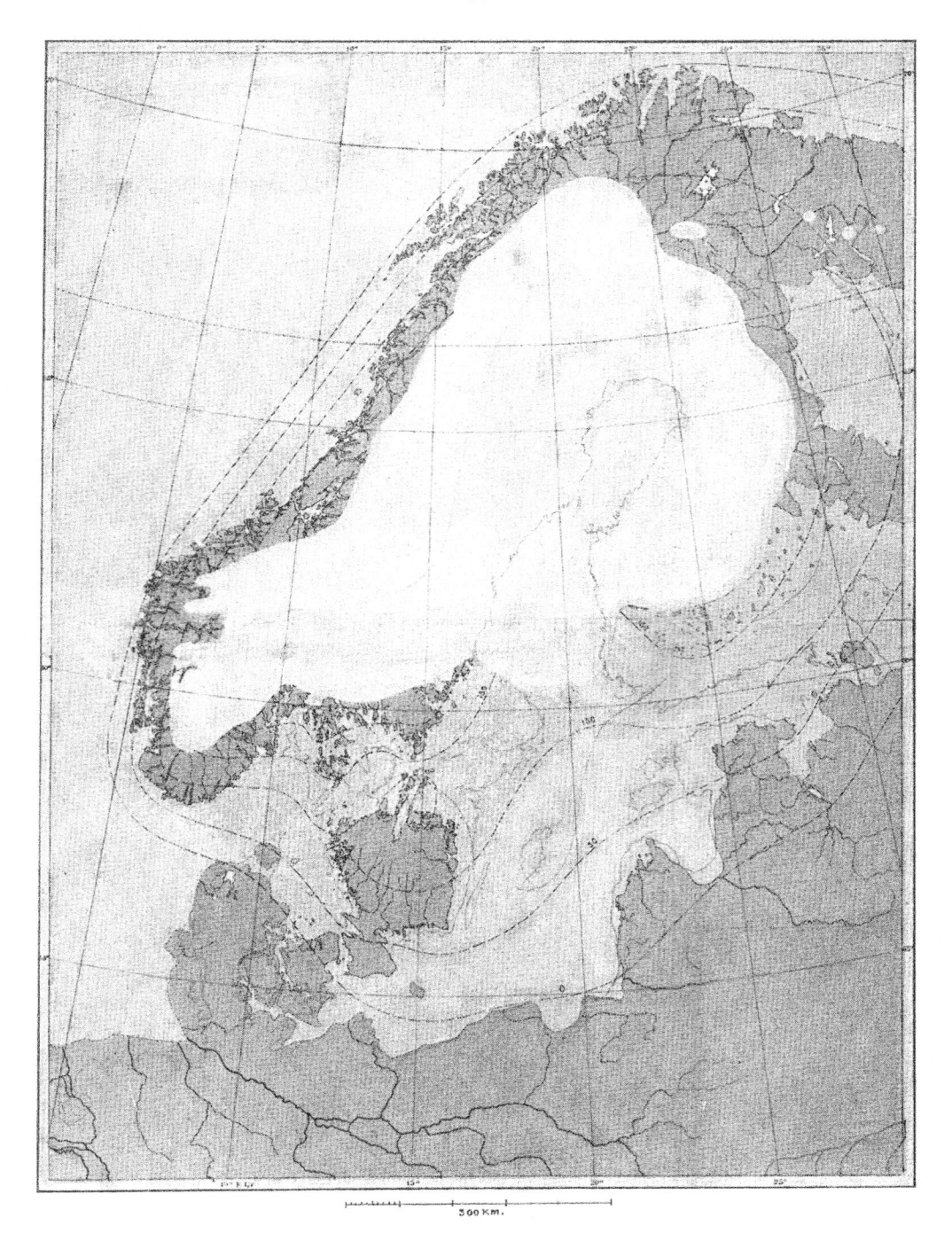

Baltic Sea Region in the Yoldia stage.
(per De Geer, *Om Skandinaviens geografiska utveckling efter Istiden*, Tab. 3).
The dashed arc lines (isobases) connect the points of equal elevation. The numbers indicate by how much (in meters) the land and sea floor are higher today than during the time of the Yoldia.

Baltic Sea Region in the Ancylus stage.
(per De Geer, *Om Skandinaviens geografiska utveckling efter Istiden*, Tab. 5).
The dashed arc lines (isobases) connect the points of equal elevation. The numbers indicate by how much (in meters) the land and sea floor are higher (or lower) today than during the time of the Ancylus.

— 88 —

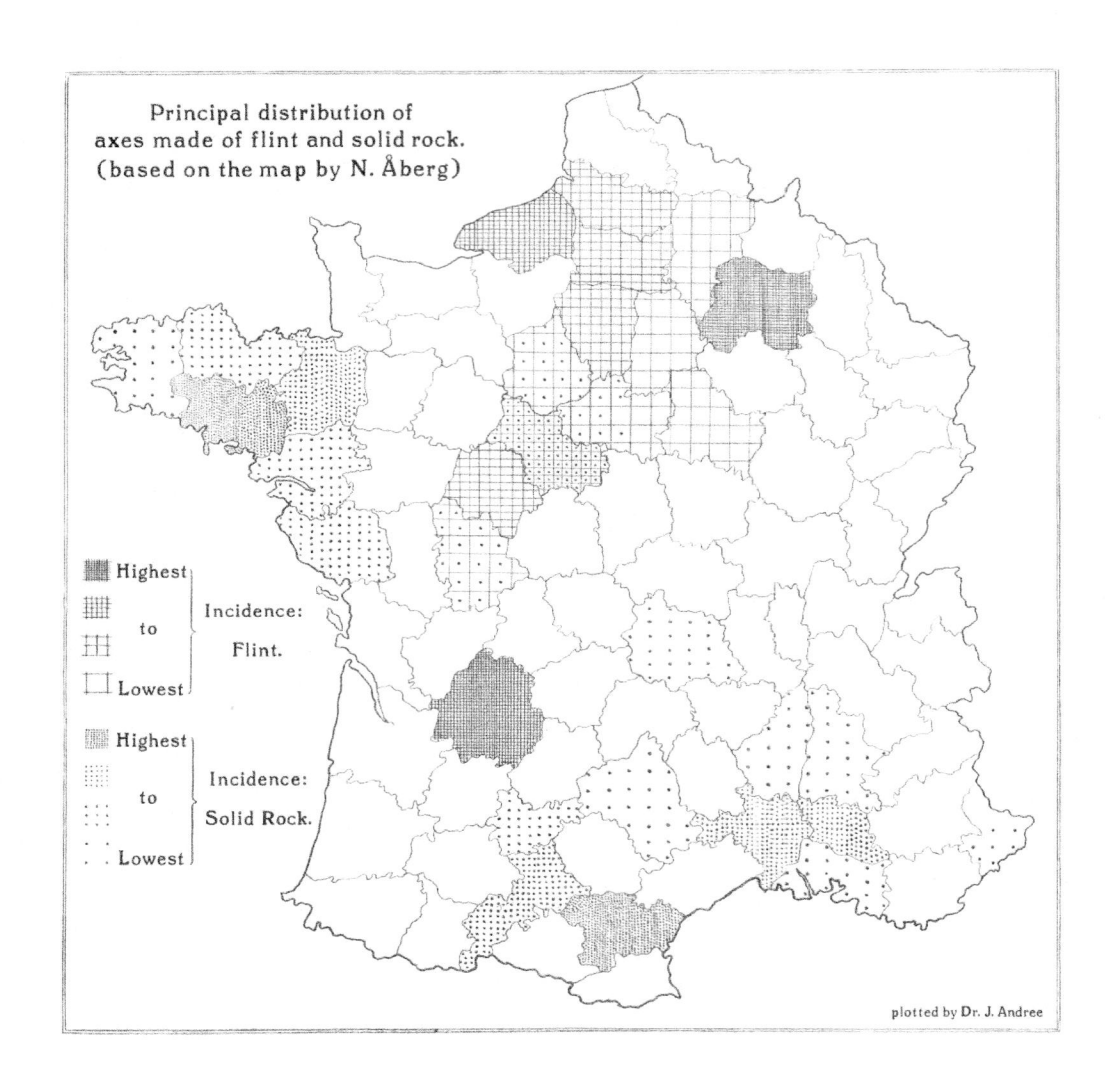

Principal distribution of axes made of flint and solid rock. (based on the map by N. Åberg)

Incidence: Flint.
Highest to Lowest

Incidence: Solid Rock.
Highest to Lowest

plotted by Dr. J. Andree

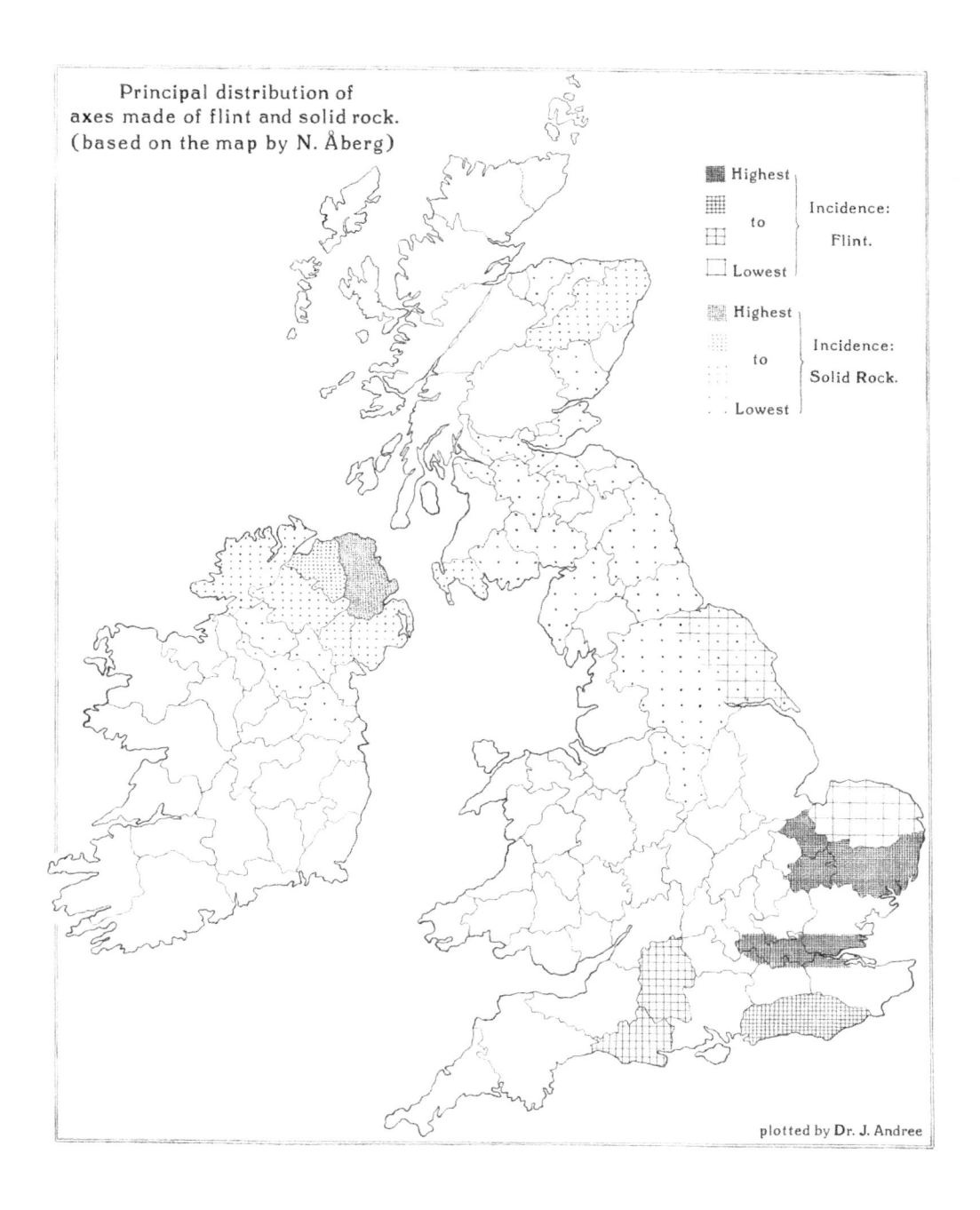

Principal distribution of axes made of flint and solid rock. (based on the map by N. Åberg)

Incidence: Flint. Highest to Lowest

Incidence: Solid Rock. Highest to Lowest

plotted by Dr. J. Andree

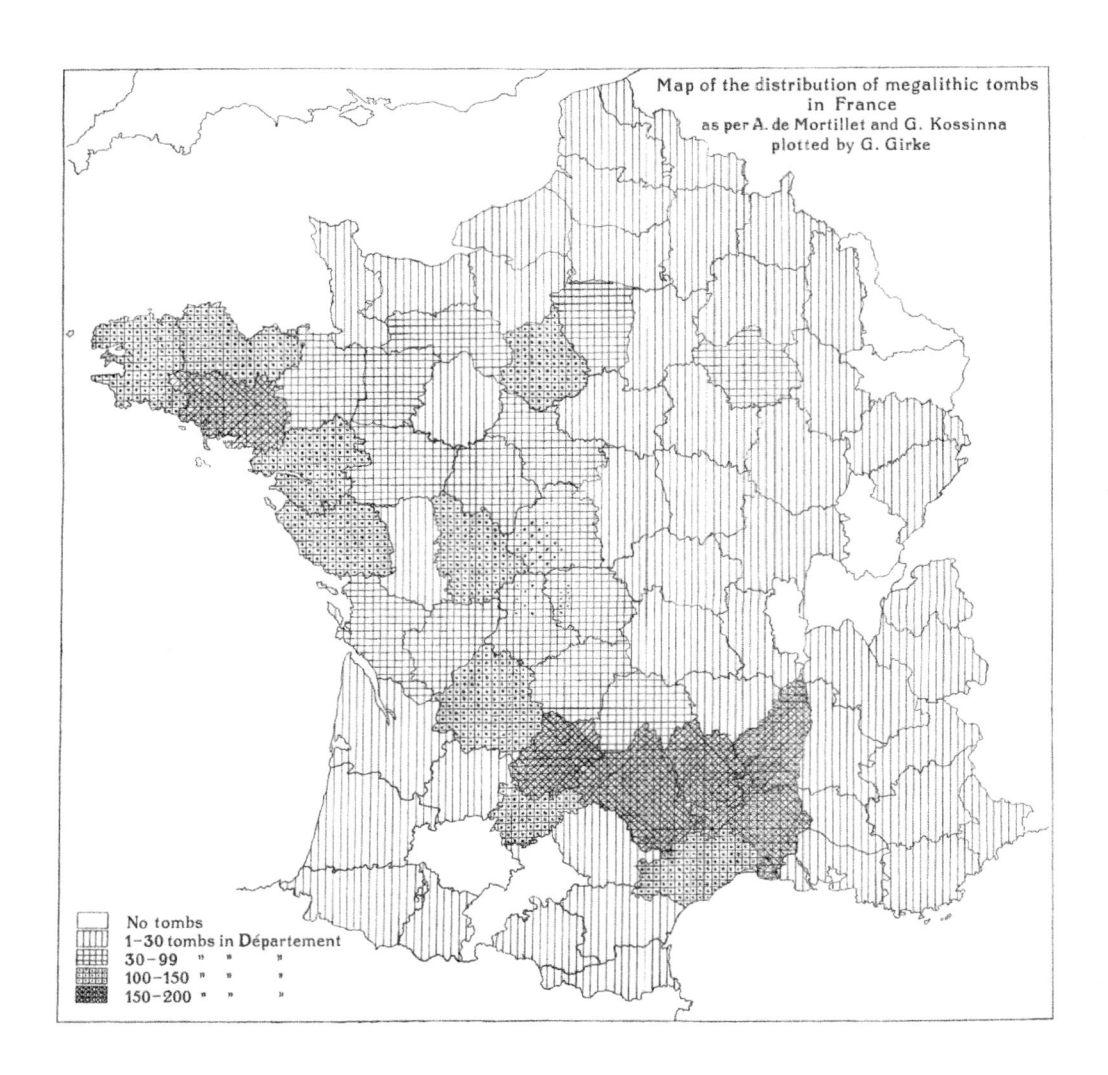

Map of the distribution of megalithic tombs in France
as per A. de Mortillet and G. Kossinna
plotted by G. Girke

No tombs
1–30 tombs in Département
30–99 "   "   "
100–150 "   "   "
150–200 "   "   "

Translator's Note

Originally published in 1921 as *Die Indogermanen - Ein Abriss, I. Teil: Das indogermanische Urvolk*, this work was originally intended to be the first part of a two-part series, as alluded to on pages 78 and 79. However, a second part of this intended series was never published. Arguing in favor of a Northern European origin for the Proto-Indo-Europeans (a view currently considered outdated) from archaeological, linguistic, and racial-anthropological standpoints, while also addressing the origins of the Finno-Ugrians, this work would go on to form the great bulk of the material referenced by V. Gordon Childe in his 1926 book *The Aryans: A Study of Indo-European Origins* in that book's discussion of Kossinna's views on Indo-European origins. Despite the lack of a direct follow-up to this book, this would not be the last time that Kossinna would touch upon the origins of the Indo-Europeans, and we intend to publish more translations of Kossinna's works in the coming years.

Just as in our previously published translation of Kossinna's *The Origin of the Germanics: On the Method of Settlement Archaeology*, the German terms *Indogermanen* and *indogermanische* were translated as Indo-Germanics and Indo-Germanic (rather than Indo-Europeans and Indo-European), which is still the dominant nomenclature in the German-speaking world. It is also important to note that the terms Pre-Indo-Germanics and Pre-Finns (translations of *Vorindogermanen* and *Vorfinnen*, which could also be more literally translated as "Fore-Indo-Germanics" and "Fore-Finns") refer herein to ancestors of the later Proto-Indo-Germanics and Proto-Finns (*Urindogermanen* and *Urfinnen*) rather than peoples who were replaced or subsumed by those groups. This in contrast to the reference to the (lowercase p) pre-Hittite Luwians, who it should be clear from the context were not described as being ancestral to the Hittites. Finally, while preparing this translation, some typographical or transcription errors were identified in the original text — these have been corrected, and the resulting corrections and other changes are listed below.

Changes

Page 15 line 14 from the bottom (including footnotes) originally read: 180:123.
Page 20 line 8 from the bottom originally read: Figs. 12, 14a, 21, 22, 26, 27.
Page 29 line 7 from the bottom originally read: Fig. 28.
Page 32 caption for Fig. 51 originally read: I owe the illustrations for Figs. 48 and 49 to the Museum vat. Alt. in Kiel.
Page 60 line 7 from the bottom originally read: Figs. 108, 110, 113.
Page 64 line 2 from the bottom originally read: Fig. 125, No. 7
Page 85 originally read: Per K. Keithark.
In general: Full initials or full names of cited authors were often added when only a surname or first initial was originally given. Full names or titles of cited journals and books were often given where only an abbreviation was originally given. Abbreviations of the names of journals were only used if said journal had already been previously cited.

ABOUT THE AUTHOR

Gustaf Kossinna was born in Tilsit, East Prussia on September 28, 1858, the son of a high school teacher. From 1876 to 1881 he studied at universities in Göttingen, Leipzig, Berlin, and Strasbourg, initially focusing on classical philology and then broadening his studies to include Germanic philology, art history, history, and archaeology. In 1881 he was awarded a doctorate by the Kaiser Wilhelm University of Strasbourg for his work on the oldest High Franconian language monuments in Strasbourg. It was his studies at the Friedrich Wilhelm University of Berlin under professor of Germanic philology Karl Müllenhoff that would inspire him to devote his career to prehistoric archaeology to pursue the origin of the Germanic people, and more broadly, the origin of the Indo-Europeans. After earning his doctorate, Kossinna spent several years as a librarian and then a curator at several libraries in Germany, and simultaneously began developing his archaeological method and publishing scientific papers. In May 1900 he was granted the title of professor by the same Berlin university where he had studied under Müllenhoff, but it was not until 1902 that he was appointed to an assistant professorship in German archaeology, a position created specifically for him.

After the death of German prehistorian Albert Voss in 1906, Kossinna had hoped to take his place as the director of the department of prehistory at the Royal Museums in Berlin, but in 1908 the position instead went to prehistorian Carl Schuchhardt, precipitating a rivalry between the two which would last for decades. When in 1909 Schuchhardt founded the journal *Prähistorische Zeitschrift* as an organ of the Berlin Society for Anthropology, Ethnology, and Prehistory, of which Kossinna was a member, Kossinna responded in the same year by founding the German Society for Prehistory (later renamed the Society for German Prehistory in 1913). The journal *Mannus* was then founded to serve as the organ of the new society, with Kossinna as editor. Kossinna would go on to write numerous publications on the prehistory of the Germanics and the Indo-Europeans before his death in Berlin on December 20, 1931. Through these publications and the development of his method of settlement archaeology, he played a seminal role in the emergence of prehistory as an academic discipline. His approach began to fall out of favor in the decades following World War II, but major advances in archaeogenetics have refocused scholarly discussion on prehistoric migrations, reviving interest in his legacy.

Printed in Great Britain
by Amazon